Developing High Performing Staff

A Retailer's Guide To Finding And Keeping The Best

Diane Abbey-Livingston
Dale D. Becks

RETAIL LEARNING INITIATIVE

Centre for the Study of Commercial Activity, Ryerson Polytechnic University, Toronto

Developing High Performing Staff

A RETAILER'S GUIDE TO FINDING AND KEEPING THE BEST

Diane Abbey-Livingston
Dale D. Becks
Diane Abbey-Livingston and Associates

Graphic design and layout: Caterpillar Graphics
Cover Design: Jacques Cantin

Developing High Performing Staff:

A Retailer's Guide to Finding and Keeping the Best was produced by the Retail Learning Initiative as part of its "Retail Smarts" project. The Retail Learning Initiative is a long-term educational program for retailers and a key part of Ontario's retail sector strategy. It is coordinated and managed through the Centre for the Study of Commercial Activity and the Centre for Advanced Technology Education at Ryerson Polytechnic University. The educational activities of the Retail Learning Initiative have been developed through the collaboration of the following groups:

Canadian Booksellers Association
Canadian Retail Hardware Association
Ontario Ministry of Economic Development, Trade and Tourism
Retail Council of Canada
Ryerson Polytechnic University

RETAIL LEARNING INITIATIVE
Centre for the Study of Commercial Activity
Ryerson Polytechnic University
350 Victoria Street
Toronto, Ontario, Canada
M5B 2K3

ISBN: 0-919351-40-9

Table of Contents

INTRODUCTION

INTRODUCTION

What does your world look like? Perhaps you are just starting out in retail for the first time, or maybe you have been in business for a while. Perhaps you are planning to open your second (or fifth) store, or you are expanding into a bigger location with more diverse product lines. Perhaps you are located in a huge mall in a metropolitan area, or on main street in a small town. Whatever your current situation, if you are interested in having your staff help you grow your business, this book is for you!

Small to medium-size retailers, like you, know their success depends in large measure on their staff. Few products sell themselves. The advantages of a great location can be lost in the hands of the wrong staff. No wonder retailers want to know the best and most time-efficient ways to develop high performing staff.

The purpose of *Developing High Performing Staff* is to answer the dozens of questions you have about finding the right staff, supporting high performance and handling performance problems. Our intention is also to raise awareness of the impact that human resource management has on the bottom line of your business.

Inspiration from Successful Retailers

Having worked in retail as well as in other sectors, we know that retail is a unique setting. So, when we began to write this book, we asked ourselves whether the standard theories about managing staff would be a good fit for your unique world. We set out to test them through in-depth interviews with retailers recommended as having highly successful businesses selling books, hardware, fashion, furniture, jewellery, provisions and equipment. In addition, we talked informally with dozens of other retailers. They inspired our writing with their responses to questions like:

   ○ How do you go about attracting new staff?

   ○ How can you tell from the interview if there's a "fit"?

   ○ How do you get staff on board quickly? How long does it take?

   ○ How do staff start to take on more responsibility?

   ○ What do you think motivates the members of your staff?

   ○ How do you develop initiative in your staff?

   ○ Do you conduct performance reviews with staff?

   ○ What advice do you have for other retailers?

The retailers with whom we spoke conveyed a rich blend of philosophy and practicality. They talked about their values and beliefs. They talked about the nitty gritty of what happens in their stores and how their values influence daily practices. Developing High Performing Staff reports their experience and thereby explains how to develop teamwork, foster learning and create on-going excellence.

Managing People is a Juggling Act

Managing the staff component of your business is like a juggling act. Juggling looks so simple when it is going well. Eighty percent of the balls are in the air at any time and everything is going smoothly when OOPS, one slips, you've lost the rhythm and they all could come tumbling down.

Your store is much the same. Everything is going well. Suddenly the administration and shipping person gets sick, and your best salesperson decides to go back to school full time. Two staff have a serious argument, a new product arrives and no one seems to know where to find the product or pricing information. It seems like it's all going to fall apart.

Depending on the day, the week or the season, you can probably handle a few of these unexpected events. The problem is that each event has a ripple effect on the others. The juggler misses one ball, loses the rhythm and everything could fall. We experience the same thing!

Is it possible to create a smoothly running operation? The retailers we interviewed said "Yes!" They told us that it takes them time to find, hire, train, coach and build a strong, productive team. They learned, some of them the hard way, that if they didn't invest the time and energy in managing their staff on a day-to-day basis, their sales and profits suffered.

As an owner or manager, you have to find a way to juggle or balance your time and energy. You have to ensure that all of the essential ingredients for a successful store are under control and supporting your goals. You need to decide what is important, and what it will be like when the right things are being done well. You must ensure that they happen – even if you are not in the store.

Will This Book Help?

If you are curious and want to know more, you will find practical ideas on how to:

○ attract applicants for openings in your store

○ interview and hire the right person

○ get the new hire up to speed quickly and effectively

○ set performance expectations in ways that motivate staff

○ develop staff skills and knowledge through coaching and training

○ develop staff initiative

○ talk with staff about their performance and their goals

○ turn performance problems into productivity

○ create and use recognition and rewards to support store goals.

We will begin with a discussion of the major functions of the store owner and manager in human resource management. Your business needs a sense of direction and it is the role of the store owner to provide leadership by determining the mission of the business and its values. It is the role of the owner and manager to ensure that "systems support success." Great staff cannot produce great results without policies and systems that are effective.

Communication, the subject of Chapters 2 to 5, is the water in which retail sinks or swims every day. Your attitudes, style and skills shape the culture and the work climate. These chapters make a case for paying as much attention to communications as to sourcing, buying, marketing and merchandising.

Communications and the Water You Swim In takes you into the bones and muscles of effective conversations. It provides a method that everyone can use to assess their effectiveness as communicators. You can teach the model to your staff and use it to help them enhance their communications with customers.

Personally, I am always ready to learn, although I do not always like being taught.

Winston Churchill

Hearing Isn't Listening, Chapter 3, puts a microscope to listening so that you can appreciate the skills that combine to increase accuracy in receiving information. Responding to emotions is the subject of Chapter 4. How to acknowledge feelings without losing the focus on achieving results is discussed and examples are provided. Once again, you can share the information to help staff deal with customers' feelings. Giving clear information is not as simple as it sounds. Chapter 5 provides you with easy-to-use tips on this essential skill.

Panning For Gold is devoted to the process of finding potential staff. The motto "Court many, wed few" metaphorically points to the need for keeping an eye out all the time. You will learn tools to help you recruit and about places to look for good candidates.

Hiring the Best takes you from the moment of screening candidates to the moment of celebrating the candidate's acceptance of your job offer. Based on a tried and true model of the interview process, you'll discover how to plan the interview and what specific questions to ask to ensure you get an in-depth picture of each candidate.

Three chapters are devoted to helping your staff develop competence and confidence. Orientation – Bringing the New Staff Up to Speed helps you plan successful entry for new hires. Coaching and Training outlines your role in developing staff knowledge and skills. Developing Staff Initiative Through Work Assignment describes a way of managing your staff so that they will take on more responsibility, and show initiative in ways that ultimately free you to grow your business.

Everyone wants to know how to deal with a staff person who is not performing well. The chapters outlined above and one other will help you avoid performance problems. Reviewing Performance with Staff invites you to consider a seasonal review with staff to celebrate successes and learn from disappointments. It works the same way as a seasonal review of sales and merchandise.

Turning Performance Problems into Productivity identifies sources of typical problems and shows you how to handle them.

The last chapters, Recognition and Rewards, and Motivation, provide insights into what turns people on and off. They offer a wealth of ideas from retailers like you.

Communication and motivation are the bookends that support the other chapters. These two areas affect everything you do. Ideas, tips and how-tos about communication and motivation appear in every section. This emphasis reflects the belief that being able to communicate effectively with your staff contributes to your ability to motivate them. As you'll discover throughout this book, nothing happens well without proper attention to communication and motivation.

How to Use This Book

Depending on where your priorities are at the moment, and what your issues are, you may want to start in the middle and jump around the chapters. Or you may prefer to start at the beginning and work your way through sequentially. Whatever approach appeals to you will work.

If you do what you have always done, you will get what you always got

Adults learn in a variety of ways so there are many options. Each chapter has self-assessment tools, theory, advice from high performing retailers, step-by-step guides for applying models, and excerpts from sample conversations. There are cases, exercises to work through, spaces to jot down ideas and action plans, and sample forms to copy. There are also a lot of questions to stimulate your thinking.

We suggest you write in the book. Use post-it notes, coloured pens, write in the margins – mark the ideas you want to remember.

Whether you are brand new to the business or have considerable retail experience, whether you are new to management or a seasoned manager, we hope you see this book as a great buffet. As you look over it, notice what appeals to you. Select a reasonable-sized meal. Unlike a restaurant buffet, you will be able to come back again and again. Also bear in mind that this meal will take a long time to digest.

In real terms, if you were to implement one idea from each chapter every month, the impact on your store's performance would be significant within six months. Now is a good time to start.

You and Your Staff – Living Assets

This chapter will:

✓ describe eight leadership roles for successful retailers

✓ identify the central role your values play in everything you do

✓ provide a way to clarify and build commitment to values you and your staff can share

✓ identify the major activities involved in managing staff

✓ enable you to assess the skills required to develop high performing staff

THE TRUTH ABOUT RETAILERS

Retailers are a unique and special breed of people.

You have a passion for your products and for providing service. You are convinced that everyone on the planet should have at least one of what you sell. You are a creative entrepreneur, working limitless hours to create the look and feel in your store that customers will love to shop over and over. You have a dedication, perseverance and an intense focus on getting the right product mix and the right staff in order to achieve your dream. Your greatest joy is to see everything working, your store bustling with activity and happy customers taking your products home to enjoy.

WHAT IS YOUR ROLE?

There are many components to your business and you are responsible for all of them. It's a big job and you choose to do it because you love the complexity, the variety and the challenge. But, occasionally, it is important to stand back from the daily demands and ask: "What is my role?"

The following is a synthesis of what we heard from successful retailers and what the literature says about the role that leaders play in their organizations.

Leaders of successful companies believe their role is to:

- ○ frame the future
- ○ seek shared purposes
- ○ honour the heart
- ○ enable staff to be successful
- ○ build a learning organization
- ○ nourish positive working relationships
- ○ promote teamwork
- ○ guide through shared values.

Frame the Future

Your unique responsibility as a leader of your business is to frame the future and decide what pictures will fit in the frame. You determine what business you are in and why. Each time you plan and purchase the assortment of products and services you will offer, you decide which customers you will target and which needs you will serve. Every decision you make about marketing, merchandising, and store operations is a step toward your dream of the business as you want it to be.

Seek Shared Purposes

Purposes are energizing and exciting when people are committed to them. People need to know and value how their work fits into the big picture. The motivation to learn and work comes from seeing the relationship between daily tasks and longer term goals -one's own and those of the business – and from believing in one's ability to contribute.

Are you building your business just to pay the bills? It must feel like that some days. But when you stand back and think about it, and when you look under the pile of bills, you will find deeper purposes. Some may be related to creating a better life for people around you. Some may be related to developing your own potential. Whatever they are, your heartfelt purposes are the source of your commitment to your business.

Your staff have deeper reasons for working than the pay cheque they get from you. Do you know what they are? Each person has purposes which are linked somehow to the work they are doing for you. Connect with the link and you will tap into a tremendous source of energy.

They will never let you down if they understand that your destiny is in their hands and vice versa.

Anonymous

Honour the Heart

Does it sound odd to say a business person should "honour the heart"? Not according to people who do research about successful organizations. Commitment comes from the heart.

Whether you picture yourself at the top or at the centre of your organization, you have tremendous power to influence the daily experience of the people with whom you work. While the way you use your power is your choice, different choices have different consequences. Over time, your kind and sharp words add up to call out or crush the motivation of your staff. It makes good business sense to use your personal power to build up your staff so that you can all be successful.

Recognizing individual contributions is part of honouring the heart. In some organizations, there is no appreciation unless the goal is achieved. So if three staff members make the sales target, they are seen as the winners. But what happens to staff who are under target if success is defined solely in terms of meeting the target? What about a staff person who increases her sales by 25 per cent but still does not make the goal? And, what about buyers or back room staff who contribute in a different way?

When you care about honouring the heart, you find ways to show staff that their contribution matters. You find ways to reward people along their journey. You look for small gains. And you also celebrate.

Enable Staff to be Successful

Leaders remove the roadblocks to success. They have the power to question and challenge how things are done. They have the power to encourage staff to do the same.

Look at the way your store operates. Have you set up effective ways to handle routine tasks? Are the procedures you have in place a help or a hindrance? Can a new person find support from you, from other staff, or by reading clearly written material?

Being clear about your expectations, so that everyone knows their roles and responsibilities, is essential to success. Providing coaching and training is part of enabling people to be successful. It also creates an organization that learns from experience.

Create a Learning Organization

A learning organization is a group of people who are committed to continuous improvement and have the permission, skills and tools to do it. As the leader, you set the tone for what can be discussed. Are staff permitted to talk about last week's results? Are they allowed to talk about last week's staff meeting? Is it OK for staff to raise questions and talk about the way people treat each other? If it makes sense to discuss sales results with a view to improving them, then it's equally sensible to review staff meetings and daily interactions.

Learning organizations have methods for getting feedback about their work. They pay attention to the information they get. They ask customers a lot of questions about what they need and what would make their shopping experience better. They ask each other how well they are working together. They are committed to ongoing learning and improvement at the individual, team and store levels.

Stimulate curiosity. Interest yourself and your staff in what customers and suppliers think about your store, the products, the service, the relationships among staff, etc.

Question assumptions and teach others to do the same. Make asking good questions a highly valued, positive behaviour by modelling and encouraging it. As staff look back on such topics as last week's sales, merchandising the store or the staff meeting, encourage them to ask questions that probe beyond: "What went well? What went poorly?" and "How can we improve?" While these are productive questions, further probing is usually needed to get to the thinking that lies beneath the way things are done. Ask: "Why are we doing things the ways we are doing them?"

Learning organizations search for new ways to do things. They set up informal experiments, asking questions like: "What happens to sales and customer service if we move this display over there?"

Commitment to learning shows in the attitude you have toward mistakes. When errors happen in your store, how do you react? Some managers say "mistakes are an acceptable part of learning," but then react in ways that convey disappointment or mistrust when an error is made.

Commitment to learning shows when people are given challenging jobs and allowed to take calculated risks. Commitment to learning also shows when coaching is a valued part of work.

Nourish Supportive Relationships

A learning organization cannot survive when there is fear and excessive competition. Fear drives candid communication away. Excessive competition leads to hoarding information and customers. You have a major part to play in fostering collaboration and co-operative effort.

Do people respect and support each other, or do they find fault and undermine each other? How about you? Do you focus on strengths or weaknesses? Do you dwell on the fact that Gary is hopeless at remembering to take out the garbage or do you remember that he always arrives early and you can count on him? It is so easy to find the negative differences between people. Have you ever heard yourself say, "I wish Gary could be more like Jessica"? Have your staff heard you say that? Perhaps the real question is: "Do you put your energy into making all the different skills, talents and personalities work together to strengthen your business?"

In any relationship, there will be tense moments, disagreements and conflicts. Your behaviour when you are around tense situations will set the tone for the staff. If you crush an idea and explain the reasons, that is very different from crushing the person who voiced the idea. You model how to handle differences.

What role do you take when conflict arises between staff members? Do you encourage them to work it out for themselves and coach each person when appropriate?

Promote Teamwork

You have many demands on your time. Between sourcing and buying product, marketing, merchandising and managing store operations, you are busy. How you juggle everything will be determined by your particular approach to managing and building your own business.

In *The E-Myth Revisited,* Mike E. Gerber describes Sarah, a high energy, capable owner-manager who worked 10 to 12 hours a day, on a regular basis, trying to do it all. She was a "Lone Ranger" who didn't have competent staff, and because of this, she didn't have the time to find them. She was caught in a vicious circle. Sarah finally realized that she would never escape the circle unless she changed. She would have to make the time to find staff, coach and train them and set up business systems to support their success.

> *Power in organizations is the capacity generated by relationships. It is real energy...*
>
> **Margaret Wheatley, Leadership and the New Science**

In *Flight of the Buffalo,* James Belasco and Ralph Stayer contrast two other approaches to building a business. One model describes the manager as "head of the herd" of buffalo. He or she takes responsibility for planning, organizing, co-ordinating, controlling and doing all the important work. The buffalo, who are loyal followers, do whatever the head buffalo commands (which is exactly what the head buffalo wants). As a result, the herd stands around and waits for the head buffalo to tell them what to do next. When he or she isn't around, things grind to a halt.

In contrast, the manager as "lead goose" is a member of a group of responsible, interdependent birds who fly well together. The leadership at the front of the "V" formation changes frequently. Each goose is alternately responsible for a variety of roles – as leader, follower or scout. In this model, the lead goose trusts and respects the others. Even if the lead goose is gone for a week, the formation is still maintained and progress continues.

You are not the "Lone Ranger," or "Head of the Herd," or "Lead Goose." But you face the same challenges they do. You must find your way to balance your need to control the business with the need to empower others. Otherwise, you risk having staff who wait to be told what to do, and losing the personal freedom to have a life outside your business.

The answer to "why don't staff take initiative?", a question we are frequently asked, is linked to you. It depends on your ability to groom individual staff and to promote a team in which people support each other and feel as responsible for success as you do.

You have staff. You cannot do it all. Encouraging them to work together is an investment in your future.

TEAM means: Together Everyone Achieves More.

Guide Through Shared Values

You determine the values that will guide your operations. Values are central to everything you do and everything you want done. Your values shape the decisions you make. If you place value on "tried and true" methods, you will be less likely to risk innovation than someone who values creativity and novelty. If you value change, you will be more likely to seek growth than if you value stability.

Values reflect what you believe to be true and important. Your values are so central to managing staff that the next section is devoted to them.

CLARIFYING YOUR VALUES

When you talk about your values, you are talking about what you believe to be important. Whether you actually speak about them or not, you have strong beliefs about how you want your business to operate and the kind of culture you want to create. You have strong beliefs about how to treat your customers, your staff, and your suppliers. You value certain ways of working.

Many companies have a statement of values posted in their stores. Some use the values as part of orienting new staff and as criteria against which they can check how they are operating.

Talking with staff about what is important is one way to move toward mutually agreed-upon ways of working. This sort of discussion draws from the heart because it is about what really matters to people. It promotes team understanding, lays the groundwork for clear expectations, and supports high performance.

Before you discuss values with your staff, explore your own. Values are so much a part of how each of us thinks and acts that it is sometimes difficult to pinpoint the ones that are the most important. The following four methods will help you think about what matters to you.

1. Think About Your Business

Use what you know about your store to give you an idea of the values that seem to be in place now. The chart on page 9 provides space for you to make notes as you consider the following questions:

○ What is most important to you in terms of how customers are treated? Is personal service important? Is store appearance important? Is satisfaction important? Is providing knowledgeable information about the products important?

○ What is most important to you in terms of staff? Do people enjoy working in your store? Is it important that they do? What is the temperature of the relationships: cold, cutthroat competition or warm enough to support both competition and co-operation? Is the climate important to you? How about the honesty index? Are people afraid to tell the truth for fear of reprisal, or do they know that they will be treated with respect and fairness? Is it "survival of the fittest" or a team that scores together by using each other's strengths and resources?

○ How do you think you should treat suppliers? What are the most important qualities you look for in your products?

2. Think About Businesses You Admire

What is it about the businesses you admire that makes you respect them? How do they treat their customers? Their suppliers? Their staff? What are the values they express in the way they conduct business?

3. Think About Businesses You Do Not Admire

Look at the other side of the coin. What is it about the way they do business that doesn't appeal to you? What behaviours do they demonstrate?

4. Examine the Values Other Retailers Have Identified as Important to Them

As you read the following samples of value statements, consider which ones sound familiar to you and which ones strike a chord in your heart. Are there some that you want to adopt as clear statements of your values?

SAMPLE VALUES STATEMENTS

Here are a few samples of value statements that retailers have developed to guide their behaviour.

- *We treat people – our staff, customers and suppliers – with dignity and respect. Our business is built on relationships.*

- *Our team is committed to excellence in all we do.*

- *We are dedicated to learning: from our customers and each other.*

- *We will not compromise on our products, staff and service.*

- *We will build a top quality team that is willing to do whatever it takes to satisfy our customers.*

- *We treat everyone who enters the store as "special."*

- *We are fair and don't take advantage of people.*

- *We are a store where fun and laughter are found.*

- *My business is built on:*
  - *relationships with customers and staff,*
  - *respect and trust in the individual,*
  - *hiring the best people possible,*
  - *investing time and energy to train them well,*
  - *opportunities for increased responsibility,*
  - *teamwork, hard work and fun.*

- *I grow my business based on:*
  - *personal service to our customers – we call them regularly;*
  - *the value added we give our customers, not the price;*
  - *turning customers into friends;*
  - *customers recognizing our commitment to excellence without us having to tell them.*

On the following chart, make notes about what is important to you. How do you want to treat your customers, suppliers and staff? What principles do you want to guide your behaviour?

CLARIFYING OPERATING VALUES

Thinking About My Business

1. How do I want customers to be treated?

2. How do I want staff to be treated by me and by each other?

3. How do I want suppliers to be treated?

4. What words do I hope staff will use to describe what it is like to work here?

5. What do I value most about the way I conduct business?

Thinking About Other Businesses that I Admire

1. How do they treat their customers, staff, suppliers?

2. What do I admire about the way they do business?

Thinking About Businesses I Do Not Admire – what specifically is it that I don't admire?

Statements from Other Retailers that I Want to Use

After you have answered the questions and reviewed the values statements from other retailers, look at your notes. Are there certain values that seem to describe what is important to you? Draft a list of between five and 10 values that you regard as essential to your business. They don't have to be fancy or long. You might think of them as operating values or guiding principles.

WAYS TO USE YOUR VALUES LIST

Once you have developed a list of values that are important to you, what can you do with it? Leaders of organizations describe the following ways in which they have used their lists.

1. Use Your Values List to Guide Your Activities

Think about your behaviour. In what ways do you demonstrate your values to your staff and customers? Do you "walk your talk"? Do you act in ways that are consistent with what you wrote?

Values are our ideals. They represent what we want to live up to. Looking at your list gives you an opportunity to:

- ◯ congratulate yourself on areas of consistency between what you do and what you value
- ◯ notice areas of inconsistency
- ◯ plan what you want to change in your behaviour
- ◯ implement your desired changes.

Although living up to your ideals is a lifetime's work, it is done one day at a time. One retailer told us he gives himself a report card twice a year. He says he is more critical of himself than anyone else and he values being honest with himself.

2. Use Your Values List to Improve Business Operations

Think about your own business. In what ways do your policies and practices demonstrate your values? Are there policies and practices that seem inconsistent?

A restaurant owner went to a workshop in which he had an opportunity to list his values. On the day that he took his list and wrote it up as guiding principles, he walked through his restaurant and heard a waiter say: "I know it's on the lunch menu but we don't make it at dinner. We make almost the same thing but we don't put it in a bun or serve the same sauce." Later the owner asked whether the waiter had explained why the request could not be met. The waiter didn't know why, as no one had told him the reason. The owner recalled an item from his list of guiding principles: "Do our best to serve you the way you want to be served," and shook his head. He made a note to explain the "why" behind policies, and to train everyone to know when and how to bend them.

> If they work for you, you work for them.
>
> Japenese Proverb

DEVELOPING HIGH PERFORMING STAFF

Think about your policies and practices related to your staff. In what ways do they demonstrate your values?

3. Use Your Values List to Develop Shared Understanding With Your Staff

Talk about the items on your list with your staff on a one-to-one basis or at a staff meeting. Post them on the wall and invite their comments.

A well-known retailer developed a values statement and circulated it through the company. One of the executives who had been involved in writing it asked people what they thought about it. He learned that few people knew about it, and those who did were indifferent. The executive decided to hold meetings with staff to discuss the meaning of the value statement. His respect for staff grew and staff were very positive about the conversations during and after these meetings. As a result, the values in the statement have come alive. Staff now use them as reference points to talk about what their culture is and what they want it to be.

4. Develop Commitment to Shared Values

The process of building a values list with staff involves 2 – 3 staff meetings in which staff work with you to develop a joint list of principles that guide work. The power of talking about values together lies in the fact that discussion matters to people, includes everyone and leads to action in day-to-day behaviour.

A step by step approach to involving staff in talking about ways of working and values is provided in Appendix I.

Your values lie at the centre of everything else you do in developing high performing staff. Whatever else you decide to do, talking about them and treating them as guiding principles for work will stand you in good stead.

COMPONENTS OF DEVELOPING HIGH PERFORMING STAFF

We have been discussing the core of developing high performing staff. This centre influences how you involve yourself in each of the human resource management activities below.

Nothing happens well without effective communication. It is the key to finding new staff and getting them on board. It is the basis for the coaching and feedback that builds staff competence, confidence and commitment. It is the medium through which you delegate, develop and discipline. Communicating effectively with staff is central to your ability to motivate them.

Developing high performing staff major components

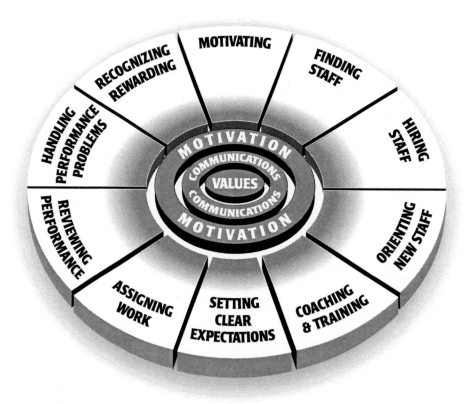

As a way to launch yourself into the rest of the book, you might like to assess your ability regarding the skills required for the activities identified above.

LEADERSHIP SKILLS IN DEVELOPING HIGH PERFORMING STAFF

Select the number that best reflects how you see your skills:

1 point = I need to improve this skill
2 points = I do this adequately
3 points = I do this well

What is your skill in:

_____ 1. Building a positive climate for work

_____ 2. Assessing my own effectiveness as a communicator

_____ 3. Drawing out information

_____ 4. Listening to what people say

_____ 5. Responding to feelings

_____ 6. Modelling the behaviour I want from staff

_____ 7. Recruiting a talented pool of potential staff

_____ 8. Interviewing to find the "fit" between candidates and store needs

_____ 9. Making job offers attractive

_____ 10. Hiring the right person

_____ 11. Bringing people up to speed by orienting them to our ways of doing things

_____ 12. Coaching people to perform at their best

_____ 13. Providing training opportunities

_____ 14. Assigning work in ways that develop staff competence, confidence, and initiative

_____ 15. Developing procedures to simplify work and maintain consistency

_____ 16. Making my expectations clear

_____ 17. Recognizing staff efforts and achievements

_____ 18. Developing effective reward programs

_____ 19. Asking for staff input

_____ 20. Dealing with performance problems

_____ 21. Tapping into staff's motivation

_____ **TOTAL SCORE**

Interpretation:

21 – 35   This book will provide you with a solid foundation
for developing high performing staff.

36 – 50   There are ideas in this book that will move you towards
greater success.

51 – 63   Some fine tuning is all that is needed.

The chapters that follow will remind you of many things you are already doing well. It will also suggest new ideas and hopefully inspire you to go out and manage what may well be the most important part of your business – the people who work with you.

How did we get to the moon? One step at a time...

[1] de Geus, Arie, *"Planning as Learning",* Harvard Business Review. March/April 1988.

Communication – The Water You Swim In

2

This chapter will:

✓ identify the two key components of any conversation

✓ point out the benefits of paying attention to these features

✓ explain how to assess your effectiveness in communications

A COMMUNICATOR'S QUIZ

Read each item on the left and check off one box that best reflects your assessment.

How do you assess yourself?	I am doing this well	I am doing this ok	I need to give this more attention	This is not relevant to me
1. I make communications with my staff a priority.				
2. Knowing that what I say and do affects productivity and morale, I pay attention to the way I communicate.				
3. I use daily conversations with staff to get the work done and build a positive work atmosphere.				
4. I express my emotions in ways that respect other people's feelings.				
5. I build and maintain positive work relationships through the way I communicate with people.				
6. I ask staff what I do that helps/hinders them.				
7. I treat staff with respect.				
8. I ask staff their opinions and seriously consider what they say.				
9. I have effective methods for keeping everyone informed of store happenings and plans.				
10. I evaluate how effective I am as a communicator.				
TOTAL CHECK MARKS				
Multiply by	multiply by 3	multiply by 2	multiply by 1	multiply by 0
TOTAL SCORE				
GRAND TOTAL - add total scores of columns 1 + 2 + 3				

Interpretation

0 – 10	Your communication leaves a lot to be desired.
11 – 20	You likely want your communications to be effective. This chapter will help you become even more so.
21 – 30	You are building the kind of positive work relationships that support success.

WHY BOTHER TO LEARN MORE ABOUT COMMUNICATIONS?

Communication is the lifeline of the retail business.

We talk to people all the time – sometimes successfully, and other times unsuccessfully. Isn't it odd that we spend so much of our waking hours communicating (at least 70 percent) and so little time thinking about how to do it better? This chapter takes you inside the bones and muscles of the most frequent form of communications – daily conversations.

Communication colours the water you sink or swim in everyday.

Retail is a people business. How many conversations do you have every day? With the variety of customers and staff you meet every day, are you continually working to be clear with each and every one of them? Are these conversations enjoyable and productive? Are you as drawn to communications with staff and customers as you are to merchandising the store?

Let's be clear – your style and skills are central to everything you do. Sales are made or lost in the quality of the conversations with the customer. Excellent staff are found through effective interviewing and developed by the way you work with them. You cannot delegate the work, bring new staff on board, coach, supervise and develop staff initiative without good communication skills. Everything you say and do matters.

Your success depends on teaching staff to use their natural talents effectively. You set the tone for the store, for the team and for the customers.

On a minute-to-minute basis, your communication impacts on productivity and morale.

When you are frustrated and short of time, what impact does this have on staff? Can your mood be transferred to them? Of course. And, can frustrated, anxious, angry, or apathetic staff communicate their feelings to customers? You bet they can and do ...even when they try not to.

Your staff wants to do a good job. At the same time, events in their lives will impact and alter their mood or concentration. Your daily communication and interaction with them is a key factor in helping them do a good job. Your receptivity to staff makes it a comfortable or uncomfortable environment.

You set the tone for the store, for the team and for the customers. Are you sending a clear and consistent message every day with every person? Do they see that you care enough about them to coach, correct and compliment them so that they can do a good job for you? Or do you communicate that they are merely tools to generate sales? By your example, are you building a team of people who will work together, be motivated and be effective? Your way of communicating is a daily dose of your principles and values about people, staff, customers and suppliers.

You are responsible for your communication.

If your staff has not understood you, you have not communicated effectively. It's that simple. You are responsible for the message that others get from you. When you realize this, you will be less likely to blame staff for not doing what you want, or for misinterpreting your wishes. You, not they, are responsible for what you get across to them.

You are the only one who knows what you mean, and you are the only one with control over the content and delivery of what you want to communicate. Further, as the person with the power, you have the strongest impact on the communication climate in your store.

Your behaviour speaks so loud, could it be sending a message that contradicts your words?

What you do speaks louder and lasts longer than any formal teaching or coaching. It does not work to say: "Do as I say, not as I do." What you consistently do shapes the environment of your store as well as demonstrates how staff should treat customers and each other.

When staff see you at your best with a customer, they learn the "how to's" of customer service and they learn that you value customers. What kind of mixed message would they get if you later turned around and spoke in a critical, demeaning way about the customers?

On occasion, have you found that you were courteous to customers but snappy with staff? How often has this happened? What do staff learn when this is the pattern? What do the customers learn when they see this happen? Are these the lessons you want to teach? What you do teaches others what you think and value.

Sales and profits depend on your staff.

We would all like to have our merchandise sell itself, but it doesn't. The way your staff communicates both verbally and nonverbally to every customer who walks through the door impacts on your bottom line. Your staff follow your lead. They treat customers the way you treat them.

Your staff need to learn how to best use their strengths in sales.

Your success depends on teaching staff to use their natural talents effectively.

Although you can probably sense how you are doing in a conversation, you probably can't describe specifically what you are doing that is making an impact. In other areas of your life, you don't have to know what makes communication effective because you don't have to explain it. However, in retail, you are in a profession that depends on your ability to understand and describe to staff what works and what does not.

Are you an effective communicator? Are your staff effective communicators? How do you assess effectiveness? The next section addresses these key questions.

ARE YOU AN EFFECTIVE COMMUNICATOR?

When you think about effectiveness in sales, you think about the goals or outcomes you want to achieve in volume and bottom line results.

In the communications area, effectiveness is assessed in the same way. You have **desired goals or outcomes** that you want to achieve. You will always have two sets of goals because there are two parts to every conversation:

the CONTENT part, the message or information – e.g. how to ring up a sale

the RELATIONSHIP part, the part that can be thought of as communication lines, which can be open, full of static or closed.

1. Desired Outcome for the Content – How much accuracy and completeness do you need?

What is the information you want to give? What information do you want to get? How important is the content and how much accuracy do you need? If you are giving instructions, accuracy is important. It is less so when you are chatting at a party with friends.

2. Desired Outcome for the Relationship – How open do you want the communication lines to be?

Sometimes you want someone's full attention. Other times, this is not as critical. If you were telling a story in a restaurant, you probably wouldn't be troubled if people mentally floated in and out and didn't give you their undivided attention. This wouldn't be the case if you were giving instructions or telling staff something of significance to you.

The relationship part of communication is conveyed nonverbally as well as through the content. Some research says that 70 percent of the meaning of a message is derived from nonverbal cues! For example, we all know not to take the words literally if, while looking distracted, someone says: "I can talk to you now." We have reservations about the sincerity of the person who, while looking over your shoulder at the other people in the room, says: "It's good to see you again!"

Nonverbal behavior... a wink, a frown, a shoulder shrug...

The nature of relationships and the openness in the communication lines are affected by past history. "Do you have the time?" can be interpreted in different ways. Can you imagine at least three different meanings? A literal interpretation is a request for the hour of the day. Another interpretation is a request for attention.

Nonverbal behavior... tone of voice, speed of speech...

How To ...

And a third, to illustrate our point, might be a flip comment by someone who sees that the watch she gave as a gift is not being worn. Nonverbal behaviour directs how you interpret the words you hear.

Given the two components of communication, and the high possibility of multiple meanings, it is important to be able to assess your effectiveness. What is the best way to do this?

After a conversation, compare what you achieved to what you wanted to achieve. This is called comparing your actual outcomes to your desired outcomes. That is, compare what you wanted in terms of the content (i.e. messages you wanted to give and get) and relationship (i.e. receptivity to listening, willingness to speak and hear) to what actually happened.

Focus on one conversation at a time. In relation to a specific conversation, ask yourself the series of questions listed below.

ASSESSING YOURSELF – YOUR EFFECTIVENESS AS A COMMUNICATOR

Consider the CONTENT part of the assessment.

- ○ What content did I want to get across?
- ○ What content did I want to receive from the other person?

Now, consider the RELATIONSHIP part of the assessment.

- ○ How open did I want the communication lines to be?
- ○ What impact did I want to have on our relationship?

The answers to these questions tell you the outcomes you wanted – your targets.

Next you have to check to find out how close you came.

You check this by comparing the actual outcomes you got to the outcomes you wanted.

Ask questions and check for understanding to find out:

- ○ Was the content received the same as the content I intended to send?
- ○ And, was the content the other person intended to send to me accurately received by me?

Watch and listen to the other person to check the openness of the communication lines and the impact on the relationship.

As you become comfortable with asking yourself these questions, you will be able to use them **during** a conversation to monitor your impact and modify your delivery. For example, you will begin to watch for nonverbal signals, and respond to them by asking questions to find out whether the person is understanding what you want to say and how they are feeling about it.

Chapter 3 describes important skills for clarifying what you hear. Chapter 4 provides tips on maintaining openness in communication lines and avoiding static on them. Chapter 5 focuses on being clear. The rest of the book will apply these skills to developing high performing staff.

Communicating accurately is complicated:

- ○ What you say to me may not be exactly what you meant to say.

- ○ What I hear may not be exactly what you said.

- ○ The meaning I take from what you said may not be the mean4ing you had in your mind.

- ○ What I interpret from your facial expressions, voice tone and volume, etc. will influence the message I got.

So, how do you avoid mistakes and misunderstandings? The most productive way to deal with communications is to recognize that the meaning is not in what you said or what you intended to say. The meaning of what you said is in what the receiver heard and interpreted.

If they haven't heard, then YOU haven't communicated what YOU wanted to and YOU need to modify YOUR message and YOUR delivery.

No matter what you want to convey (desired outcomes), you are stuck with what your receiver actually got (actual outcomes), until you modify your content and delivery.

BUILD AND MAINTAIN A POSITIVE CLIMATE

How do you make sure the water you, your staff, and customers swim in is clean and clear? You do this over time using communications that:

- ○ demonstrate good will and respect

- ○ treat staff fairly

- ○ clarify what is expected

- ○ invest in success by providing coaching and recognition

- ○ invite and consider staff ideas

- ○ provide the most positive working conditions possible.

Positive relations are formed as one conversation after another takes place in which there is mutual respect and consideration. These qualities are expressed through attentive listening, asking questions, rephrasing, and acknowledging

feelings (skills described in detail in the next three chapters). Within any one conversation, the relationship is built and monitored by **paying attention to the response you get and by modifying your content and delivery** (e.g. pace, tone, volume, etc.).

SYSTEMS SUPPORT COMMUNICATIONS

Positive relations are also supported by the systems you have in place that demonstrate what is important to you. You are busy. You can't attend to everyone all the time. What methods do you use for ensuring that everyone knows what is happening all the time?

Daily News and Plans

Some stores use a daily calendar book in which staff record the happenings on their shift. Not only does this provide the next shift with everything they need to follow up on, it provides you with background to analyze sales. Staff record:

- ○ supplies that are low, or have run out
- ○ customer compliments, challenges and complaints
- ○ problems (merchandise, fixture, staffing levels)
- ○ current events that may have affected sales (mall event, parade, snow storm).

Customer Service Reminders

Some stores put customer service reminders into the daily calendar book. Other stores, that have the technology, use a memo pad feature at the point of sale terminal. As a sales person rings up a sale, the memo pad reminds them of something each day: "Smile"; "Ask the customer if they have enough replacement light bulbs and fuses."

Procedures

A procedure is a **clearly described method** for doing something that is to be **used by several people, consistently,** throughout the store. This is most useful for activities which are:

- ○ routine, frequent, predictable tasks
- ○ somewhat complex
- ○ related to security or safety
- ○ time-consuming or problematic if errors occur
- ○ done by different people

SYSTEMS

Procedures are helpful in areas like:

○ Receiving a shipment

○ Ringing up different types of sales

○ Completing a return, exchange or refund

○ Opening the store

○ Closing the store

○ Taking inventory

○ Taking telephone orders or messages

○ Dealing with theft or shoplifting

○ Dealing with emergencies (fire, accidents, etc.)

Appendix II describes how to develop a procedure so that it is effective and so that staff are committed to implementing it.

Sales Motivation and Recognition

Some stores have goal boards at the back of the store and each staff person tracks sales per shift.

Some stores post consumer thank-yous where they can be seen by all staff.

Some store managers leave a recognition note on a bulletin board.

Some stores have a weekly memo that provides sales results and congratulates top performers.

Some list every store, the average per store and each staff person's results in relation to the average for the store in which they work.

Product News

Several stores produce informal newsletters that have product information, changes, plans and thank-yous. One store puts the newsletter in biweekly pay envelopes: another leaves copies out where customers can also see them.

What do these systems provide? Predictability. Staff and management know where to go for some specific, concise information. **Important? Yes. Sufficient to create success? No. Success depends on face-to-face discussion.**

Success depends on face-to-face discussion.

Your Attitudes and Your Skills

The three most important factors in creating healthy communications are:

○ your attitudes and beliefs about your staff

○ your communication skills and flexibility

○ your willingness to learn.

If you believe your staff have skills to offer, ideas of merit, and can learn to be even better at what they do, read on to find out more about tried and true communication methods that will help you build your team.

If you believe that learning continues throughout one's life and that the end of formal schooling is only one phase of the journey, then you know that you will continue to develop your capacity to be a better communicator and manager.

Perhaps the greatest challenges to productive work relationships lie in managing our differences and the daily conflicts that arise because of them. Perhaps the greatest danger to our business lies in not discovering the differences between us that would, if we communicated effectively, lead to new and better ways of doing things.

The building and maintenance of any relationship is an ongoing process. It never ends.

REALITY CHECK

If a neutral third party asked your staff to comment on your communication skills, what would they say? How would your staff describe you as a communicator?

You may find it interesting to go back to the quiz at the beginning of this chapter and anticipate how your staff would respond to each item. To get a picture of how you think staff would answer, fill the form out again with an "s" to indicate their perceptions. Do you think their perceptions coincide with yours?

Even better, reproduce the assessment and ask each member of your staff to fill it in, anonymously, with you in mind.

Provide an envelope where staff can return their responses without identifying themselves.

Then, summarize all the responses to see the pattern of their perceptions. When you have summarized their responses:

○ What do you like about what you see?

○ Is there anything you would like to ask staff about?

○ Is there anything you would like to change?

○ What can you learn from your staff that will make you more effective?

Hearing Isn't Listening

3

This chapter will:

✓ invite you to "come to your senses"

✓ identify three essential listening skills

✓ describe the impact of nonverbal behaviour

✓ offer tips on asking questions to draw out the information you need

✓ provide examples of a way to ensure accuracy in communications

USING YOUR "COMMON SENSES"

Research indicates that you spend a minimum of 35 percent to 45 percent of your time in conversations. How effective are you? Are you using your "common senses"?

The most underused listening and communication resources are our eyes, ears and brains. We go on automatic pilot – we talk without thinking about what we are saying. We are so wrapped up in thinking about what we want to say next, or we are so busy doing something, we forget to look at the people with whom we are talking to see if they are listening.

The most underused communication resources are our eyes, ears and brains.

How Do You Know the Impact You Are Having? Are You Using Your Senses?

Jade dealers in the Orient know the impact of what they are saying and showing by watching how the client's pupils contract and dilate in response to different gems and pieces of jewellery. They have honed the common sense of seeing into a highly sharpened skill.

Though we all respond to cues **when we see them,** most of us do so without being aware of it. We all have the resources, but do we use them as well as we could?

Do you "read" your customers? What do you look for when making a sale and can you describe, to your staff, what you watch for? Do your staff focus their visual attention on the product or on the person with whom they are dealing?

Your staff pick up how preoccupied you are and what kind of mood you are in from your face and your body language. They are alert to you because you are the boss. Are you as alert to their nonverbal signals? Do you see the subtle shifts that could tell you how they feel about what you are saying? As a conversation goes along, do you monitor the impact you are having? If not, you have no immediate way of assessing your effectiveness, and thereby limit it.

YOUR EARS AND MORE – FOUR ESSENTIAL LISTENING SKILLS

Listening is more than hearing. It is an active process that involves four skills:

1. Demonstrating you are listening

2. Asking questions

3. Clarifying what you have heard

4. Acknowledging feelings.

Before looking at each of the first three skills in depth, try out this self-assessment quiz. (The fourth skill is the subject of the next chapter.)

A COMMUNICATOR'S QUIZ

Please rate yourself on each of the statements below using the following scale:

1 point = rarely
2 points = some of the time
3 points = most of the time

_____ 1. I am a good listener.

_____ 2. My customers would rate me as a good listener.

_____ 3. My staff would rate me as a good listener.

_____ 4. I look at people when they are speaking with me.

_____ 5. I am good at noticing nonverbal cues.

_____ 6. I ask questions that draw out the information I want.

_____ 7. I check that I have understood what staff wanted to communicate.

_____ 8. I am skillful in clarifying the meaning of what someone says to me.

_____ 9. I am good at recognizing opportunities for creative problem solving.

_____ 10. I listen as an interested ally.

_____ **TOTAL SCORE**

Interpretation:

10 – 16   You are missing essential information and closing down communication lines.

17 – 23   Lack of consistency on the communication lines can be confusing to the people around you.

24 – 30   You obviously recognize the value of listening.

WHAT DO LISTENING SKILLS DO FOR YOU?

Listening skills help you:

Develop positive relationships.

When you listen in a way that demonstrates you are listening, you send the message that you are willing to give your attention to that person, and what he or she is saying. You show respect. Relationships tend to be more positive when people think that they are important enough to be heard and considered.

Clarify that you have correctly understood both what was said and what was meant.

Given the many factors that affect message sending and receiving, there is a high likelihood of misunderstanding. The sender might not say exactly what he or she means. You might not hear what the sender says. The words used may have different meanings for each of you. You need methods, like the ones described in this chapter, for checking the accuracy of your understanding.

Draw out new information.

When people take the time to ensure each understands the other, new information often emerges.

Manager: *Why did you take your break at noon? I thought you knew I was counting on going to the bank at noon? You usually go at 12:30?*

Staff person: *I thought you said to take my break at noon because you knew that a new shipment would be arriving at 1:30. I didn't realize you wanted to go to the bank at noon.*

Manager: *Actually, I didn't know when the new shipment would be in. I need to make sure I read the messages and get that kind of information. Thanks for explaining why you took an early lunch.*

Staff person: *The last manager wouldn't have asked me why I did something he didn't expect. He would just be angry. I'm glad we cleared this up.*

Reduce the number of conflicts that result from misunderstandings.

"Oh, is **that** what you meant! Why didn't you say so?" Often we think we are saying what we mean, but we need the other person to ask questions to help us refine our message.

When you listen, you learn

SKILL 1: DEMONSTRATING YOU ARE LISTENING

Getting the correct content is not all there is to communication. Nonverbal behaviours convey just as much as the words. The expression, "Your behaviour is speaking so loud, I cannot hear your words," highlights a contradiction between words and actions.

Research shows that 70 percent of the meaning of a message is derived from nonverbal cues: tone of voice, speed and pitch of speech, loudness and body language. As a manager, you are required to juggle many balls at one time. When it comes to listening, stop juggling! Focus. Concentrate on the person and their message. It will save you time, energy and aggravation later.

The nonverbal listening behaviours that are easiest for you to control are:

○ making eye contact

○ smiling

○ nodding your head

○ shifting your face and/or your body toward the speaker.

Looking like you are listening doesn't mean staring or sitting opposite someone in a frozen position. In fact, in most normal conversations, you shift between taking in information and tuning out. The latter is done to think about and make sense out of the information you have already received. When you tune out, your eye contact and facial expressions change and you unconsciously let others know (IF THEY ARE LOOKING) that your lines "are busy" and that further information will not be processed at this time.

Fairly rapid shifting of your attention does not damage communication lines; it is expected. However, a consistent pattern of listening without appearing to be listening will create permanent static on the wires and make it difficult to get effective information exchange.

> *70% of the meaning of a message is derived from non-verbals*

questioning is the key ingredient in selling.

Do the daily pressures and interruptions lure you into trying to accomplish something else while listening to your staff? Does this work? On a sustained basis? What would your staff say about your willingness to listen? Would they describe the listening environment as healthy or suffering from malnutrition?

SKILL 2: ASKING QUESTIONS

The best way to get information is to ask questions. The best way to clarify and extend what you know is to ask questions. The best way to stimulate thinking and learning is to ask questions. The best way to demonstrate interest is to ask questions. Asking questions is important.

John Lawhon in *Selling Retail* says that **questioning is the key ingredient in selling.** The single most important question in every salesperson's vocabulary should be "Why?" "The phrase 'Do you mind if I ask you why?' should be a reflex response every time a customer raises an objection."

Customer: *That model won't do.*

Salesperson: *I'm sure you have a good reason for saying that. Do you mind if I ask you why?*

Customer: *I need it smaller.*

Salesperson: *Hmm... smaller... May I ask you why you need it smaller?*

Lawhon says that any time a salesperson is faced with a request to which she must say "no," finding out "why" this request is important should immediately come to mind as a question to ask. The answers might lead to creative problem solving.

Customer: *Can I have this by Wednesday?*

Salesperson: *Can you help me understand why Wednesday is important to you?*

Customer: *Do you have Brand X?*

Salesperson: *I'm sure you have a good reason for requesting this brand. Can I ask you why?*

Imagine the same principle applied to objections that staff raise to your requests. Imagine how much more you could learn, without losing your right to say no, by asking questions. Trying to understand gives you information, maintains positive relations and keeps the communication lines open.

Staff person: *Our displays aren't working the way they should. I want to change them.*

Manager: *We haven't got time this week because of all the markdowns that have to be done.*

The manager has closed the conversation without learning anything. Would the manager have been any better off if he'd asked a few questions before making a decision? Here are three approaches:

Manager: *1. Why do you say our displays aren't working the way they should?*

2. What do you think we would have seen by now if the displays were working?

3. How would you change them? What would these changes do that the current displays are not doing? Why would that work? How long would that take?

The attitude of inquiry is what your staff need to learn from you. They will learn to ask better questions as you show them how.

Sometimes you want a simple "yes" or "no" answer to a question. You want very specific information. Did Mr. Jones call? Did the shipment arrive? Did the customer buy the red ones and do we have to order more? What time are you leaving?

Other times you want more information. You want to understand what someone is thinking, or you want to hear about their experience, or learn more about a situation. When this is what you want, use open-ended questions. That is, ask questions that cannot be answered with one word. Open-ended questions often start with:

WHAT, WHY, OR HOW

Of course, when you ask a closed question to gather specific information, you can follow up with an open question to learn more about the area.

- ○ *Did you show the customer these products?* (closed)

- ○ *How did you explain these products and what did the customer think of them?* (open)

Knowing the difference between open and closed questions and being able to ask both types appropriately provides the key to interviewing, coaching, training and supervision. Indeed, the ability to ask questions is the key to creating a learning organization – an organization that seriously asks:

What happened?

What are our strengths? What needs improvement?

What else can we learn? How can we do this better?

The art of asking questions is so important in developing your staff and in customer service that we will return to it again in Chapter 7 (selection interviewing), Chapter 9 (coaching and training), Chapter 10 (developing staff initiative through work assignment), and Chapter 13 (handling performance problems).

The attitude of inquiry is what your staff need to learn from you.

See also chapter 7

SKILL 3: CLARIFYING WHAT YOU HAVE UNDERSTOOD – REPHRASING

What is Rephrasing?

How do you know that the meaning you draw from what someone says is the meaning that the person intended to give? How do you know that you understood not only the words, but also the significance? Rephrasing is an important skill to check your understanding.

When you rephrase, you state what you think you heard someone say to you. Rephrasing states your interpretation.

Listen to the meaning instead of to the words.

Why Use Rephrasing?

Rephrasing increases effectiveness in communication. It maintains or builds relationships and increases accuracy in the exchange of information.

Let's say I give you my opinion on something: "I like the look and feel of those display windows better than these." When you rephrase by telling me what you think I meant:

○ you show me you're **listening and paying attention,** which makes me feel that it is worthwhile talking to you

○ you help me **check and modify my message** so that it conveys the meaning I want it to. Only by hearing what you have understood will I know what to modify.

When to Use Rephrasing

Rephrasing opens up communication lines. This is useful when there is tension, conflict, or confusion. It is essential when you want accuracy – for example, in giving and receiving instructions, coaching, problem solving, and interviewing.

Introduction to Examples of Rephrasing

Each example that follows looks at part of a conversation. Even if the examples don't use words that you would, they can give you ideas about how to use rephrasing.

As you read the examples, you may find yourself asking questions instead of rephrasing. Chances are, your questions would be useful. The purpose here is to illustrate rephrasing. Being able to use both skills provides you with flexibility.

Content +
Relationship =
Communication
Effectiveness

Example: Dealing With Objections

Manager: *When a customer raises an objection, before you reply to it, I would like you to rephrase your understanding of what the customer said.*

Salesperson: *If I just repeat what the customer has said, I'll sound like a parrot!*

Manager:
(Rephrase 1) *It does seem strange to tell someone what you think they just said.*

Salesperson: *You got it. I don't want people to think I'm stupid or making fun of them.*

Manager:
(Rephrase 2) *I can understand that. When I talk about rephrasing, it sounds strange. I don't want a customer, or anyone for that matter, to think I'm mimicking them.*

Can you imagine this conversation? How is the manager doing? Is he clarifying the meaning of the salesperson's concern? Is the manager keeping the communication lines open?

This is a typical situation where someone is asking someone else to do something. When the person disagrees, we are often tempted to respond by justifying our request. Here, the manager avoided this temptation. Instead, he chose to **demonstrate interest** in the other person's point of view.

Manager: *Have I got your concerns about rephrasing clear?*

Salesperson: *I think so.*

Manager: *I certainly don't want you to think I have been parroting you. But, I have been rephrasing my understanding of what you said to make sure I understood what you meant. How did it come across to you? Did you think I was making fun of you? Did I "put you off"?*

Salesperson: *Actually, I didn't notice what you were doing. I thought you were getting my point. I wasn't turning off to it.*

Manager: *Good. I was getting your point without putting you off. And that's just what happens when you rephrase the objections back to customers. The customers feel that they have been heard. Then you can go on to respond to their concerns.*

Note: The manager is demonstrating the skill he wants the salesperson to use.

"Rephrase the objection to ensure you understand before you respond to it."

Example: Incorrect Interpretations Can Lead To Shared Understanding

Owner: *I've noticed that some of the salespeople sell merchandise instead of customers. They don't realize customers give all kinds of information from the moment they walk into the store and during the entire sale.*

Manager:
(Rephrase 1) *So, you think the staff spends too much time at the back, or straightening things instead of watching the customers.*

Owner: *Not exactly. I was thinking more of what sales people miss during the conversation.*

Manager:
(Rephrase 2) *The example I think of is when a salesperson shows one piece of merchandise after another and doesn't notice that the client has tuned out.*

Owner: *Exactly – that's an example. Some of them don't watch the impact they are having. They don't pay close enough attention to the client's reaction. They fuss with the goods instead.*

Notice that the first time the manager rephrased, he had not understood what the owner meant. His interpretation enabled the owner to modify her statement to better communicate what she meant.

Remember, **there is nothing wrong with an incorrect interpretation** when it leads both people to clarify what they mean.

Rephrasing focuses on the message already sent. The purpose is to clarify content or open communication lines, not to switch to another topic or point of view. However, sometimes an incorrect interpretation does introduce a new topic. When it does, pursue the new topic if it helps you understand the other person's views. Do not pursue the new topic if it draws the speaker to your views. Switch to your views after you have understood and confirmed your understanding of the other person's views.

Example – Avoiding Premature Conclusions

Manager: *I need some help. I'm having a real problem getting Paul to do what I say.*

Owner:
(Rephrase 1)
When you give him instructions or ask him to do something, he just doesn't do it?

Manager: *Well no. It isn't that he doesn't do the job. It's that he does it his way despite the instructions I've given him. And, his way is wrong. What should I do?*

Owner:
(Acknowledgement)
(Rephrase 2)
I want to answer your question, but before I do, let me make sure I understand what has been happening. You have been giving Paul instructions about how and when to do a specific job; later you find that he has done the job but not according to your instructions.

How many people do you think would have been "hooked" into trying to answer the manager's problem immediately?

The trouble with answering right away is that the owner might offer a solution before really understanding the problem. Imagine what the owner might have advised if he had used his first interpretation as his understanding of the problem.

The problem could be:

○ the way the manager gives instructions – the content of the instructions or the way the content is delivered

○ the instructions are wrong and Paul knows it

○ Paul is unwilling to be supervised by the manager.

To get a better understanding of what the manager is referring to, the owner will likely ask an open question such as: "To give me an idea of what is happening, can you tell me what you said to Paul the last time you gave him instructions to do something?" or "I'm wondering what specifically you told Paul and what he did that was different to what you told him to do?"

Notice that the owner avoided premature conclusions. His acknowledgement of the manager's question, at the beginning of the last statement above, demonstrated that he heard it and did not intend to ignore it. This acknowledgement generally has a reassuring effect and therefore maintains open communication lines.

Your staff need to learn the discipline of avoiding premature closure: "No, we have none." They need to learn how to respond to a customer's question in a way that enables them to learn more about the customer's needs. They need to use the same steps as the manager used in the examples on the previous page:

> ## UNDERSTAND THE QUESTION BEFORE YOU ANSWER IT DON'T GET HOOKED
>
> ○ acknowledge the question ("I want to answer your question.")
>
> ○ commit to answering ("...before I do, I'd like to ask you a question...")
>
> ○ and rephrase and/or ask for more information.

The patterns of communication that you use provide living examples for your staff, especially if you can describe what you are doing and why it's effective. Teach your staff the steps above and use examples from this book to explain why these steps are effective.

LISTENING AS AN ALLY

This chapter has been about three listening skills: demonstrating that you are listening, asking questions, and rephrasing. These are the bones and muscles of listening. The head and heart come from your attitude.

When you talk with some people, you get the impression they are open to you and your ideas. They seem to come from a position of wanting to understand and join you in considering whatever you are talking about. These are people who listen as allies. They create a work climate in which people try to help each other, look for better ways to do things, and help each other succeed.

When you talk with other people, you get the feeling they are poised to find fault, disagree or defend themselves. They listen as adversaries. They breed caution, unhealthy competition and stifle creative thought.

Does an ally ever say "no" or disagree? Of course, but only after considering the person, their views and possibilities for accommodation.

REALITY CHECK:

How would a neutral third party score the assessment at the beginning of this chapter after observing you for a few days? How would staff respond if you asked them to complete the assessment with you in mind?

Listening as an ally is a choice. All it requires is desire and a disciplined focus on your communications. It is a wise investment in creating a learning organization.

HOW DO YOU LISTEN TO EACH OF YOUR STAFF?

List Staff Persons' Names	How I Think I Listen		How I Think The Person in Column 1 Would Say I listen	
	mostly as an Ally	mostly as an Adversary	mostly as an Ally	mostly as an Adversary

ACTION PLANNING

What ideas from this chapter do you want to remember?_____

_____

_____

_____

What do you want to START DOING?_____

_____

_____

_____

Is there anything you want to STOP DOING?_____

_____

_____

_____

No doubt there are many things you want to continue to do. Too many to write here. Are there two to three behaviours you want to highlight here to CONTINUE TO DO?_____

_____

_____

_____

_____

_____

_____

_____

_____

_____

_____

_____

Listen to the Melody as well as the Lyrics – Respond to Feelings

## 4

This chapter will:

✓ make a case for responding to feelings

✓ enable you to express caring without compromising your standards

✓ indicate times when you might forget to acknowledge someone's feelings

✓ describe ways to respond to someone's feelings when they have made a mistake or when you don't approve of their behaviour

✓ provide guidelines on acknowledging feelings

A COMMUNICATOR'S QUIZ

Please rate each of the statements below using the following scale:

1 point = rarely
2 points = some of the time
3 points = most of the time

____1.   I remember that emotions affect someone's **ability** to work.

____2.   I remember that emotions affect a person's **willingness** to work.

____3.   I respond to feelings as if they are a valuable source of energy.

____4.   I monitor how I express my feelings.

____5.   I communicate to customers that I care about them.

____6.   I communicate to staff that I care about them.

____7.   I pay attention to the emotional climate of the store.

____8.   I am skilful in acknowledging feelings in conflict situations.

____9.   I am able to listen and respond to feelings without having to give up what the store needs.

____10. I treat people with respect.

____   **TOTAL SCORE**

Interpretation:

1 – 10   Read this chapter and discover a whole world that impacts on your success.

11 – 20   You don't have the responsiveness that one finds among high performing retailers yet.

21 – 30   You're creating a climate that is conducive to developing staff potential and store success.

WHY ACKNOWLEDGE FEELINGS?

To Have Feelings Is To Be Human

"When you come to work, leave your personal life at home." " While you are at work, keep your feelings in check." " There's a time and a place for everything." Have you ever heard these statements?

Do these statements sound like you? Or, do you believe that while each of us monitors what we express at work, our feelings are always with us. Often they sneak out in tone of voice, and other non-verbal messages and remind us of their presence. We choose how and when to express them but they are always present.

Feelings Indirectly Ask for a Response

Have you ever told someone something that was exciting to you and their response indicated disinterest? Did you feel let down? Disappointed? Confused?

Children and teenagers have this experience often. They come home and joyfully report about some event – a prank they played, or an invitation they received. Parents recognize potential problems and immediately say: "You shouldn't have," or "You can't go."

To the child or teenager it feels like a wet blanket has been thrown. Most react to criticism or decisions like the ones above by arguing and this reaction is intensified by the sudden shift in their feelings (from excited or happy to defensive or angry). Inevitably they say:

"YOU DON'T UNDERSTAND!!"

Their response would be less intense if parents showed respect and caring by acknowledging the feelings of the child or teenager before criticizing or saying "no." The same truths apply when we are dealing with our adult friends, partners, associates and staff.

Feelings Lead the Way

When you are excited about something, you have energy. When you are frustrated, you also have energy. The question is where to direct the energy. Frustration with some aspect of how the store operates can be an invitation to create innovation. Or, it could be something that everyone continually grumbles about. The choice rests in your response to the feelings.

Acknowledgement of Feelings Feeds Many Motivational Needs

The major theorists of motivation suggest that people have a "hierarchy of needs." At the basic level, the need for safety and security guides the choices people make. Fear of ridicule erodes a staff person's willingness to express a new idea or maybe even their ability to be honest!

Think about it. Whose feelings do you tend to ignore?

The next set of motivating needs has to do with affiliation or the need to belong. These needs are what drive people to behave in ways that ensure they are included in the group. Does the staff team value high performance or do they set unspoken limits? Whatever standard the group sets, people try to meet it.

The need for recognition includes the need to be seen as unique and the need to have achievements acknowledged. When you ignore their feelings, staff assume that you view them only as tools, not people.

WHAT IS ACKNOWLEDGING FEELINGS?

Acknowledging feelings is responding with words or actions to the emotions expressed by the person with whom you are talking.

Sometimes people tell you directly how they feel about a situation, about themselves or even about you. Other times, their feelings are indirectly expressed through their tone of voice, speed of speech, facial expression and body language. However feelings are expressed, there are many different ways of responding to them. Here are some of them.

1. Asking Questions

Asking questions can open communication lines, show interest and obtain more information.

○ *How did you feel in that situation?*

○ *You sound excited about that. Are you?*

○ *Some people would be pleased about that, others would be skeptical. What about you?*

2. Sharing Similar Experiences

When someone tells you about an experience, you could share the feelings you had in a similar situation. When you do this, and if your purpose is to show that you are interested and that you understand, keep your story short. When you say a lot about your experience, you will switch the attention to yourself and unwittingly appear to be more interested in yourself than in the other person.

○ *When a situation like that happened to me I felt ... I wonder how you feel?*

○ *Although I didn't have the same reaction as you, I sure can understand how someone could feel the way you are feeling.*

3. Imagining How People Could Feel

Even when you have never experienced a particular situation, use your knowledge about how people you know felt in similar situations.

○ *I know that ... can happen and when it does some people feel excited, and others feel nervous. I wonder how you feel about it?*

○ *Although I have never experienced that myself, I've heard others say that they feel ... What's your reaction?*

4. Rephrasing With a Similar Tone

Rephrasing is particularly useful to demonstrate that you are listening, to obtain more information or to confirm feelings.

○ *From what you have said, when X, Y, and Z all happen at once, it can really leave you feeling frustrated or ...*

5. Sending Nonverbal Messages

Through gestures, nodding, facial expressions, changing your tone of voice, etc., you can demonstrate that you care.

WHAT ABOUT YOUR FEELINGS?

In one day you may ride the roller coaster from joy to anger and back again. Your feelings are real, and need to be acknowledged.

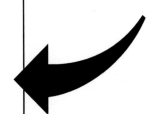

For example:

○ *I am really tense right now and need a few minutes to cool off. Can we talk later?*

○ *I need to tell you about the great applicant I just interviewed. Can I tell you about her now?*

○ *I am really focused on this paperwork and can't listen to you very well right now.*

○ *I am in a hurry and need to give you some important information before I leave. Will you stop and listen please?*

Can a System Help You?

Yes. Of course. With so many demands on your time a system can be helpful. One creative retailer introduced a method to help her staff and herself set priorities. They agreed to prioritize needs on the basis of the importance and urgency. Phone messages, notes, and hand signals indicate:

Priority 1: very important and urgent (respond within ten minutes or right now)

Priority 2: important but not urgent (respond before the end of the day)

Priority 3: important but can wait for a day or two

Priority 4: important but can wait until next week.

A phone message or note might be, "This is a P2 and I need to talk to you by 8 p.m. today."

Could a system like this help you and your staff better respect each other's priorities while trying to meet store needs? If so, invite your staff to help you develop the categories. Test the system out for a few weeks and then review it, with your staff, to ensure it is working the way you want it to work.

Introduction to Examples of Acknowledging Feelings

There are many ways to acknowledge feelings. The next section provides sample scenarios to illustrate some of them. We start with examples where it is easy to respond to feelings, but with daily pressures, we sometimes forget to do so. We then provide examples of situations when it is somewhat more difficult to acknowledge feelings. The examples focus on situations where:

1. Something good has happened for someone

2. Someone is doing something he or she dislikes

3. Someone has tried to do something and made a mistake

4. You do not approve of someone's behaviour and his or her performance must change

---

DESIRED OUTCOMES FOR THE EXAMPLES

In each example, we are assuming that the Owner/Manager has the following desired outcomes for the conversation:

○ To continually build a positive working relationship

○ To keep communication lines open

○ To clarify the meaning the situation has for the other person.

The focus here is on acknowledging the feelings of your staff. This is also relevant to acknowledging customers' feelings and teaching your staff to do so.

1. Acknowledge Feelings – When Something Good Has Happened

The best selling book, *The One Minute Manager* by Ken Blanchard, gives the following guideline to being an effective manager:

"Catch Someone Doing Something Right" and give positive feedback.

Positive reinforcement is powerful. It motivates people in a much stronger way than traditional, authoritarian methods (that is, methods that look for mistakes, catch people and correct them). When good things happen, as in the example below, some managers see and respond to them. Others do not.

The manager is working on sales records when Peter, a salesperson, comes by and says: "Did you see that sale? He bought all three suits! That's the biggest sale I've ever had!"

Manager 1: *That's terrific. Did you make out a Customer Service Card?*

Manager 2: *Great. Nice work. You remind me of the first big sale I ever made. I think I sold a suit, two shirts and a tie and I was really excited. How do you feel?*

Manager 3: *Great. Nice work. You know when someone buys that much it's important to check that you have marked all the alternations correctly. Perhaps you'd better check them.*

Manager 4: *That's terrific. Tell me how you did it?*

Your choice is?

Which Manager's response is most like what you would say in this situation? Which is least like you?

Manager #   is most like me.   Manager #   is least like me.

Managers 1 and 3 do recognize the positive accomplishment. However, in terms of the number of words, and the time it would take to say them, the recognition is minimal. Much more time is spent on looking for mistakes or "teaching" the sales person. It is unlikely that Peter will believe either managers' praise, or feel acknowledged.

The responses of **Managers 2 and 4** recognize the positive accomplishment in a way that will probably be heard and felt by Peter.

While Manager 2 doesn't draw out details about the sale, the response certainly lets Peter know that he or she shares his excitement and understands how he might be feeling.

Manager 4 encourages Peter to talk about the sale and may even help him learn more about what he is doing that is effective. This response is a good example of "learning from doing," which is a hallmark of a learning organization.

2. Acknowledge Feelings – When Someone Is Doing Something That They Don't Like Doing

Which of the statements below do you believe best describes your view?

Your choice is?

> ___At times, everyone faces conflicts between satisfying personal work preferences and meeting store needs. Staff are usually more concerned with their likes and dislikes than with doing what the store needs to be successful.
>
> ___At times, everyone faces conflicts between satisfying personal work preferences and meeting store needs. Staff usually do what is needed to make the store successful.

If you checked off the second statement, you are starting the development of staff commitment and high performance from a positive base.

When you ask people to do tasks you know they don't like to do, acknowledge their feelings.

Manager: *I know you don't like to clean the windows. Knowing how you feel, I appreciate the fact that you do it thoroughly.*

Manager: *I know that you were upset when you had to rearrange several things to come in today. I appreciate that you did it even though it was a problem for you.*

Some managers might ask, "Why should I acknowledge their feelings or thank them when it's part of their job?" Other managers know that you support someone's commitment by:

○ recognizing performance

○ acknowledging preferences

○ building positive relationships.

When people are asked to do tasks that don't provide satisfaction or enjoyment, the relationships they have and the recognition they receive are important.

You build relationships through conversations and the recognition you get from them. One conversation will not break a relationship. However, a pattern of not acknowledging feelings, over many conversations, will have serious consequences for morale and productivity.

When was the last time you provided recognition to someone who made a mistake?

3. Acknowledge Feelings – Even When Someone Makes a Mistake

What do you think each person in the last frame was thinking? What would you say to the salesperson?

This manager seems more interested in the salesperson's failure or his possible failure than in his success. Either he doesn't know very much about motivating staff or he is having a bad day. Whatever his reasons, his behaviour does not demonstrate good staff relations.

In the dialogue that follows, the manager recognizes that he does not have to choose between acknowledging feelings and correcting performance; he can do both. Notice how he combines his response to the salesperson's feelings with recognizing the achievement, motivating performance and correcting the mistake.

Manager:	*That's fantastic! Tell me, how did you do it?*
Salesperson:	*Well, first I showed him .... Then I ... and then ... I felt great when he decided to buy it all.*
Manager:	*You did a really good job there. I like the way you showed the two items and compared the features and benefits. The customer looked pleased.... (PAUSE) By the way, what ID did you check?*
Salesperson:	*Oh no! I forgot. I guess I was so pleased it went clear out of my mind.*
Manager:	*I can see you are upset about forgetting. I know that you realize how important it is and that in the future, you will remember. Do you think a procedure is needed to remind people to ensure that IDs are checked? ... (LISTEN) ... While this was a fairly serious error, you can still be very proud of the sale you've made.*

In businesses where the owners and managers are committed to improving operations, they try to learn from experience. In this case, the manager would follow up to assess the extent of the problem in checking I.D. The manager would focus, not on Peter the individual, but on the bigger picture of how the store had been handling IDs. Have people been forgetting to check? If so, who? All staff? New staff? Staff on a particular shift? Is there a procedure? Is it effective? Is better orientation needed? Would reminders at staff meetings help? Would coaching?

For the purpose of illustrating a different scenario in the example above, assume that the problem was a recurring one. This salesperson had been forgetting to check on many occasions. The manager might say:

> *I really want to congratulate you on the sale and share your excitement. I can't really do that when I'm concerned that you get so excited during a sale, you forget about security. I don't want to put a damper on your enthusiasm. (PAUSE) At the same time, after forgetting three times in two weeks, I want you to improve your performance. Put as much professionalism into the security as you do into sales. Please handle this right away.*

4. Acknowledge Feelings – Even When You Don't Approve of the Behaviour

Yesterday Marie, the manager, had a terrible day. There was a problem with the cash register; a shipment arrived; a staff person, John, left early with a severe headache; and a new salesperson came in. In the middle of all this, a customer came in and was rude. Marie became annoyed and answered the customer in a sarcastic and inappropriate manner.

The customer complained to you, the owner. This morning, you called Marie and told her about the customer's complaint. Marie admitted she had been unprofessional, described the pressures of the day, and explained that she had lost her "cool."

Here are three responses. Which one do you prefer? Why?

Response 1: *No matter what is going on around you, you cannot let it affect customer service. We don't want to turn customers away and we don't want staff to think that they can behave this way. You should be demonstrating a professional way of serving customers.*

Response 2: *I can imagine how much activity there was with the shipment arriving, the cash problem, John leaving and the new fellow arriving. I know how the pressure can build up.*

Response 3: *If you had delegated more of the tasks to John and the new fellow, perhaps the pressure would not have built up that way. Looking back on the day, what could you have done differently?*

When these responses were shown to 160 managers, almost all of them preferred Response 2. They said none of the other responses communicated understanding by the owner.

They thought Response 1 sounded insulting, like a teacher or parent scolding a child. They figured that 99 percent of managers would know that customer service comes first, and that leadership on the selling floor is very important.

Tone of voice and body language would shape the impact of Response 3. The managers had mixed opinions about this one. Many thought it communicated blame just as much as Response 1, but did so in a more subtle way. Others thought it was a useful problem solving approach if used after the owner acknowledged the manager's feelings and communicated understanding of the situation.

Responses 1 and 3 deal with the content of the situation and the behaviour of the manager. While the content is very important and certainly needs to be dealt with, keeping the relationship lines open is central to dealing with the content.

Keep in mind that if you and another person are in two different places (emotionally and geographically) and you want to talk, you will have to get a connection. Acknowledging feelings begins to open the lines and build the relationship.

Notice that the owner in Response 2 is not saying he approves of, or agrees with the way the customer was handled. The owner is simply saying that he can imagine the situation and appreciate the feelings that could develop.

As a communicator, **you always have choices.** You can:

(a) Respond to the **BEHAVIOUR** (what the person did or did not do and the potential consequences)

(b) Respond to the **FEELINGS**

(c) Respond to the **FEELINGS** and the **BEHAVIOUR.**

With high demands on our time, we may be tempted to choose (a). Used on a repeated basis, (a) increases the chances of being seen as management that does not understand or care. Further, to focus only on the content, without regard for the feelings, is something like a pitcher throwing the ball at a catcher who is distracted by the action on first base.

Managers often avoid (b). They seem to be concerned that if they respond to the feelings, the other person won't take the situation seriously and they will not be able to deal with poor performance.

You don't have to choose between (a) and (b). You can address both the feelings and the behaviour. **Option (c) gives the best chances for building relationships and acting responsibly.** It is the best combination to demonstrate that management cares about both the person and the job.

CARING FOR THE PERSON AND THE JOB

Responding to feelings and behaviour works best in the sequence described below.

1. Without judging, acknowledge the feelings.

2. Clarify the situation. Ask what happened.

3. Address the behaviour. Make your concerns or requirements clear.
   For example:

○ *As I said a couple of minutes ago, I can appreciate how you felt and how difficult the situation was. How do you feel about the way you handled the customer?... (LISTEN and then, if necessary continue with)... While I understand how you were feeling, the way you expressed yourself and dealt with the situation was not acceptable because...*

○ *Now that I understand what happened, I can imagine how frustrating it was for you.... (PAUSE)... At the same time, what could you have done at that point?... (PAUSE)... There are other ways to deal with frustrating experiences like that one. For example....*

○ *Even though I do not have the same opinion as you, I can understand your thinking. I appreciate that you felt... (PAUSE)... Can you accept the way you handled the situation? Next time, which one of these alternatives do you think would work better?*

ADDITIONAL GUIDELINES ON ACKNOWLEDGING FEELINGS

Here are five points to remember when you are responding to someone's feelings:

- ○ Your assumption of how someone feels might not be correct.
- ○ Don't tell people how they should feel.
- ○ Pause after you have acknowledged feelings.
- ○ Repeat your acknowledgement until you are certain it was heard.
- ○ Make time to acknowledge feelings.

1. Your Assumption of How Someone Feels Might Not Be Correct

The visual signals that you associate with a particular feeling can mislead you. **In fact, different feelings often have similar outward appearances.** The nonverbal expression of anger can be very similar to the outward appearance of feeling frustration or pressure or stress. Similarly, boredom, intense concentration and thinking can look the same.

Making an assumption about someone's feelings can be a useful starting point if you remember that your interpretation is not necessarily correct. Whether you ask questions to check out your interpretation, or talk about feelings explicitly, or try to respect them in an indirect way, **be open to changing your interpretation.** Ask yourself the question, "What else could this mean?"

2. Don't Tell People How They Should Feel

What is your response when someone tells you: "You shouldn't feel that way"? Even if you agree, your feelings are what they are! You don't need to have someone criticize you or suggest alternative ways to feel – e.g. guilty, apologetic or embarrassed. Pushing yourself to change simply drives your feelings underground. You have a right to your emotions whether or not you express them directly. If you choose to express your feelings, you decide the most appropriate way to do so.

3. Pause After You Have Acknowledged Feelings

After you have acknowledged feelings, or rephrased what you have heard ... PAUSE ... to allow the other person a few seconds to absorb what you have said.

4. Repeat Your Acknowledgement Until You Are Certain It Was Heard

Have you ever seen a customer continue to be angry even after a salesperson has expressed concern, understanding, and offered help? Have you ever responded to someone's feelings and been surprised or frustrated when they continued on as if you had not said anything at all?

Sometimes, saying something once is not enough! There are two reasons you may not be getting through. First, check out your tone of voice, facial expression and body language to ensure your message is believable. **"I'M NOT ANGRY"** rarely conveys calm openness!

The other reason you may have to repeat yourself is static on the other person's wires. When someone is angry, hurt, or even excited, they can be so preoccupied that they don't actually hear what you say. In these situations, you need to acknowledge their feelings or rephrase what you have heard several times before it gets through. Or, try again later when they might be more receptive.

You may be wondering how long you should pause or how many times you should repeat yourself. No one can give you a formula. The signals that you have been heard and understood will be reflected in the other person's tone of voice, how fast they are speaking, and through eye contact.

5. Make Time to Acknowledge Feelings

Acknowledging feelings does not have to take a lot of time. Just as acknowledging a customer can take less than one minute, so can acknowledging feelings. In fact, most of the time, people do not need or want to go into detail about their feelings. They simply want you to show them that you understand.

Salesperson: *Yesterday was so busy, I forgot to ... I'll do it at noon today.*

Manager: *I guess you were really tired when you left.*

Salesperson: *Sure was! Anyway, I've got a lot to do now. Better go serve that fellow.*

Sometimes, someone will want to talk further and you will sense that the discussions will take time. On most issues, people accept it if you cannot take the time right at that moment.

Make time for feelings

Manager: *I sense you are concerned about this .... I'd like to talk further, but I don't have any time now. How about this afternoon around four o'clock?*

Manager: *I can see that you have a lot of enthusiasm and attachment to that idea. I don't want to crush your enthusiasm by saying "no" and I do have to say "No." I want you to understand my reasons and be sure that I understand yours. Can we meet tomorrow at ...?*

How would a neutral third party, perhaps a customer, after observing you for a few days, describe your responsiveness to feelings if they used the quiz at the beginning of this chapter? How would staff respond if you gave them this quiz form and asked them to fill it out with you in mind?

If you ignore feelings, it only makes them go underground, and develop into low morale and time-consuming, disruptive behaviour. Make the time to pay attention to feelings; you cannot afford not to.

ACTION PLANNING

What ideas from this chapter would you like to remember? _____

_____

_____

_____

_____

What would you like to START DOING? _____

_____

_____

_____

_____

_____

Is there anything would you like to STOP DOING? _____

_____

_____

_____

_____

_____

No doubt there are many things you want to continue to do – too many to write here. Are there two to three behaviours you want to highlight here to CONTINUE TO DO?

_____

_____

_____

_____

_____

_____

_____

Did They Get It? Were You Clear?

5

This chapter will:

✓ describe how to give feedback an essential skill for coaching and training staff

✓ guide your efforts in asking for and receiving feedback, essential skills for improving operations and performance

✓ identify ways to maximize the learning of your staff by combining the skills of asking questions and giving feedback

✓ provide tips on sending clear messages including communicating clear expectations to staff

✓ encourage you to practice these skills and teach them to your staff.

CLEAR COMMUNICATIONS

Have you asked for help selecting a wine or gourmet coffee lately? If so, you were probably asked whether you wanted it "with or without a bite," "high or low in acid," "smoky" or "mellow"! These terms are confusing. They mean different things to different people. How many sales staff in stores you visit use jargon when they talk to you? Do they seem to be aware they are not getting through to you?

Your staff may find your requests for "courteous" customer service and "attractive" displays as vague as the descriptions for unknown wine or coffee. Being clear is not simply a matter of choosing the right words. It takes time, attention and skill to create clarity.

Your staff want to be successful. Their ability to reach their goals in your store depends not only on the ability and skills they bring with them, it depends on:

(a) Your ability to give staff clear messages about their impact on others.

   This is called "giving feedback" and is essential to skill development.

(b) Your ability to stimulate thought and creative thinking.

   By combining questions with giving feedback, you create a powerful tool for stimulating learning. This combination of skills will be outlined and pursued in greater depth in chapter 8 (orienting staff), chapter 9 (training and coaching) and chapter 10 (delegating work).

(c) Your ability to ask for information about your skill and impact.

   This is called "asking for feedback" and its application to growing you, your staff, your business and yourself will be described.

(d) Your ability to give clear messages when you are giving instructions or communicating your expectations.

   Before getting into the meat of these matters, assess yourself via the communicator's quiz on the next page.

A COMMUNICATOR'S QUIZ

Read each item on the left below and check off the box that best reflects your assessment.

How Well Do You Think You Do the Following?	I am doing this well	I am doing this ok	I need to give this more attention	This is not relevant to me
1. I help staff learn from what they do.				
2. I provide helpful criticism.				
3. I use a variety of methods to tell staff about the impact their behaviour has had on the customers or on other staff.				
4. I ask staff for their opinions on how to improve the way we do things.				
5. I check on the clarity of my messages.				
6. I ask staff how I am helping them and how I might be getting in their way.				
7. I help staff discover how their behaviour impacts on what they want to achieve.				
8. I stimulate staff to think creatively about problems.				
9. I balance giving advice with helping staff discover their own resources.				
10. I let staff know what I expect in terms of the results they achieve.				
TOTAL CHECK MARKS				
Multiply by	multiply by 3	multiply by 2	multiply by 1	multiply by 0
TOTAL SCORE				
GRAND TOTAL - add total scores of columns 1 + 2 + 3				

Interpretation:

0 – 10   High potential for mistakes and misunderstandings.

11 – 20   This chapter offers you an opportunity to grow your business, your staff and yourself.

21 – 30   You have the foundations to build a stronger performance from your staff.

GIVING AND RECEIVING FEEDBACK

Ever wonder how bats can fly through a maze of tightly stretched wires? Or how porpoises can swim at astounding speeds and avoid obstacles in dark water? These animals use the same system. They send out sound waves which bounce off the objects around them. The sound that rebounds back is called "feedback" and it enables the animals to correct their course.

Thermostats work on the same principles. The thermostat senses the temperature. If it is too high, it turns the furnace off: if it's too low, it turns the furnace on.

Note that in these examples there is a defined "target," a goal, a desired outcome. The bat and porpoise have a direction in which they want to go; the thermostat is set to a desired temperature.

We also send out signals. Every time we speak we have an intention, a purpose, although we may not always be conscious of it. The salesperson who talks to the customer while preoccupied with folding sweaters has some intentions. While it may look like his intention is to keep the merchandise neat, his intention might also be to make a sale. If the salesperson were to watch the customer and ask questions, he would get feedback on the impact of his behaviour on the customer and on which intentions he was achieving. For the unaware salesperson, you can be the feedback system.

No wonder some coaches and elite athletes have said:

"Feedback is the Breakfast of Champions"

Feedback can make us more aware of **what** we do and **how** we do it, and the impact of our behaviour on others. Feedback increases our ability to modify and change our behaviour and to become more effective in our interactions with others.

GIVING HIGH QUALITY FEEDBACK

Here are some specific tips for giving high quality feedback:

1. Set the stage – telegraph your intentions.

2. Be specific not vague or general.

3. Describe what you saw and heard.

4. Link the behaviour to outcomes.

5. Provide the feedback sooner rather than later.

6. Check out the impact and understanding of your feedback.

1. Set the Stage – Telegraph Your Intentions

Let the person know what you want to talk about so that they can shift their thoughts from whatever they are doing to your topic.

○ *You asked for my observations on your selling skills. I have some which are based on your conversation with the last customer.*

○ *I'd like to compliment you on some work I saw you do. Is this a good time?*

○ *I'd like to tell you what I saw and heard when you were helping that customer and the impact it had on me. Do you have a moment now?*

2. Be Specific, Not Vague or General

Generalities like "staff should take initiative" can mean different things to different people. One person might think he was taking initiative by arranging to deliver a product to a special customer. Someone else might think the salesperson was over-stepping his authority in making the decision without asking the manager's permission. What specifically would you want to see staff do if you said "I wish my staff would take more initiative?"

Terms like "always," and "never," are vague. Contrast the two statements below. The first illustrates how vague terms can lead to arguments about whether something happens "always", or often or only today. You can get distracted by trying to come to agreement on the frequency, instead of focusing on the behaviour and impact. The second statement is far more effective.

○ *You always monopolize the customers! Other staff don't get a chance.*

○ *You have approached seven out of the last nine customers that walked in. Staff say they are not able to approach them because you take over right away.*

3. Describe What You Saw and Heard

"You do such a great job" might be nice to hear but it doesn't provide much information on what you think is great about the job done. It would be far more effective to say:

○ *I noticed that you got the customer to hold the product, try out the features one by one. And it seemed, from the bits I heard, that you were discussing how it would solve the problem she is having with ... Great job!*

"The sweater display is not attractive the way you have done it" provides your opinion but does not explain what you see that you think is unattractive. It would be far more effective to say:

○ *The sweaters are grouped by size which may be helpful. But, I do not find it attractive when the colours are mixed up. There is more visual impact when they are grouped.*

4. Link the Behaviours to Outcomes

The purpose of feedback is to relate behaviour to its impact on the desired outcomes – the goals. Bats and porpoises use the information gained from feedback to help them correct their direction. It's more complex in a store. Behaviour impacts on a variety of desired outcomes: overall goals for the store, your personal goals, and the staff person's goals.

When you are specific with staff by describing the impact their behaviour is having on you or the store and then giving them a reason, they are more likely to pay attention. Try the model with your staff. Teach it to them so they can use it with each other and with you.

Here is an easy, three-step model to help you remember to express yourself in a way that is specific, descriptive and related to outcomes.

LINK BEHAVIOUR TO IMPACT

1. **Describe the Behaviour.**

   ○ *When you do such and such...*

2. **Describe the Impact.** Explain how the behaviour affects you, or the staff, or the customers, or the store.

   ○ *The impact on me is... or I feel...*

   ○ *I want to...*

   ○ *The impact on staff is...*

3. **Describe "Why" the Behaviour Has Impact.**

   ○ *When you are late, the impact on me is that I can't set up the displays because I have to cover for you. The store loses opportunities to interest customers in the new merchandise and I lose opportunities to serve customers at the busy times.*

   ○ *You have been late three times this week. Our windows have not been competitive with the new merchandise because, in covering for you, I have not had time to change them.*

   ○ *When you smiled and said "Thank-you," as I saw you do with your last customer, his response was a smile too. Nice way to end what seemed like a long sale. He'll probably return because he left with a positive feeling.*

   ○ *When you fixed the merchandise for Jan I felt really pleased by the team approach you and she take (because) I value helpful relationships.*

Sometimes, when you link behaviour to outcomes, you add the consequences of continued behaviour.

○ *Is this the third sale you have made over $50? You are making records this week. One more and you get a bonus of $10.*

○ *This is the third time this week I have asked you not to tie up the line with personal calls. Yesterday we agreed that there were five calls for you. This is the third today. I've asked you whether there is an emergency or unusual situation and you have said "no." If this continues, I will give you fewer hours ....*

Don't threaten to do something more harsh than the behaviour merits and certainly don't threaten with something on which you will not follow through.

5. Provide the Feedback Sooner Rather Than Later

"For the past three months, I wanted to tell you about the problems caused by the way you have been doing the ...." The person receiving this will no doubt feel angry that you have held onto this information and in so doing, have prevented them from doing a better job. Or, the person might infer, based on the time delay, that the problems are not important.

6. Check Out the Impact and Understanding of Your Feedback

The possibilities for misunderstanding are many. Check that the content and relationship outcomes you wanted to achieve have been attained.

○ *I want to make sure that I've been clear with you. So, would you tell me what message you are getting from me?*

○ *Let's make sure that we are both walking away from this discussion with the same understanding of what has been said. I'd like to hear what you are taking away from this discussion.*

Giving Compliments – A Special Case in Giving Feedback

"Oh, it was really nothing." "I was just lucky." "Well, I had a lot of help."

Are these typical responses you have heard when you have given someone a compliment? Have you noticed that most people switch the subject soon after receiving a compliment?

Compliments can be one of the basic ingredients for developing staff and providing recognition. Use them to promote learning by heightening staff's awareness of their behaviour and the impact of what they have done. Learning takes place when you engage the person in talking about their experience. The model below works well for giving a compliment.

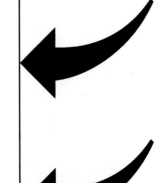

How To...

GIVING A COMPLIMENT

1. **Call attention to the situation.**

   Describe the Behaviour.

   ○ *The way you handled that sale was very effective....*

2. **Provide evidence – high quality feedback and therefore validation.**

   Explain, Using the Word "Because", How or Why You Are Making Statement #1.

   ○ *I say this because I watched you offer co-ordinates to go with the jacket he was looking at. As you presented each shirt and the turtle neck, I could see the customer really thinking. Your timing was good.*

3. **Invite ownership of the skill. Asking the person to think about what they did will promote learning.**

   Ask a Question.

   ○ *I always want to highlight the thinking that goes into effective communication. I'm wondering what was going through your mind as you were serving him?*

   What were you thinking of?

   ○ *That was a huge shipment you unloaded. I'm impressed because you put it away so quickly. Did you have a plan of attack or some special methods? How did you do it?*

WHY BOTHER GIVING FEEDBACK?

Before trying to learn these tips, think about how effective you are now. Could you be more effective? Will the effort of learning be worth it? We think so because:

- ❍ Feedback is the breakfast of champions – it's how we grow.

- ❍ We need each other as mirrors to know how our communications are impacting on each other.

- ❍ Using the skill of giving feedback directs attention to behaviour rather than to evaluations or criticisms.

- ❍ Feedback demonstrates that you are paying attention and that you value your staff.

- ❍ Feedback helps to make your compliments more believable – they are not just generalities. It's hard for anyone to dismiss a compliment with "He's just buttering me up," or "she talks that way to everyone," when it contains very specific, recent information.

Asking Questions + Giving Feedback = Staff Competence and Confidence

ASKING QUESTIONS AND GIVING FEEDBACK DEVELOPS STAFF INITIATIVE

Feedback has been defined as information that helps you see how close you are to achieving the outcomes you want. You help staff connect what they are doing to their goals by asking:

- ❍ *What were you trying to achieve with that customer when you walked through the lumber area?*

- ❍ *When you took out the two mysteries on the best-seller list, what did you hope would happen?*

- ❍ *When you walked away to answer the phone, what did you expect the customer you were talking with to do?*

In response to the question: "What did you hope to accomplish?" the salesperson might have had a clear purpose. In this case, you'd rephrase what you heard as the purpose and ask a couple of questions:

- ❍ *Do you think your purpose was achieved?*

- ❍ *What did you see the customer do or what did you hear the customer say that tells you whether or not the purpose was achieved?*

- ❍ *What might you do next time to achieve this purpose?*

Through this type of questioning, you guide staff to be more conscious and thoughtful about their intentions and actions. Depending on the answers, you may or may not want to give feedback on what you saw and heard and the impact it had.

And, what if the sales associate did not have any purpose in mind? This is a perfect opportunity for you to do some coaching.

○ *When I walk through the lumber area, I use the time as an opportunity to ask the client more about what they are planning to do, and I make comments about the different types of lumber we are passing. After the first comment, I check to see if they look interested, or I ask them if they want me to continue. It helps me learn more about them and it demonstrates to them that I know the products and can help them make good decisions.*

The first few times you try these questions, you may feel a little awkward. So will your staff. Give yourself and your staff permission to muddle through and be a little uncomfortable as you learn this valuable skill. You gave yourself this kind of permission when you first rode a bike and drove a car. Look where you are now!

ASKING FOR FEEDBACK

Whenever you want to know if the other person has understood what you meant and whether the communication lines are open, ask for feedback. There are several times when it is especially important:

○ when you have been giving instructions

○ when you have coached someone on how to do something

○ when you have given someone feedback on what they have done

○ when you have asked for a change in behaviour

To ask for feedback ask the same questions you used on page 63 to check your impact. For example:

○ *There are so many possibilities for misunderstanding in a conversation like this. Help me check how clear I've been by telling me, in your own words, what you heard.*

○ *Just to be sure I have been clear, what have I asked you to do?*

○ *Sometimes I can be very clear, and other times I am not. Please tell me what you think I have said so that I can be sure I have said what I mean.*

There are many situations in which you want to ask for feedback on events rather than on conversations. For example, you can learn a lot and improve operations by asking:

○ *What went well last week? What could have been done better?*

○ *What am I as your manager doing that helps you in your work and what am I doing that gets in your way?*

○ *What did you like about the last staff meetings? How specifically could they have been improved?*

○ *In what ways are we demonstrating our values about how to treat customers and each other?*

○ *How specifically is the procedure making the work more efficient, and in what ways is it ineffective?*

When you ask for feedback, be prepared to receive the information you get:

○ Don't get defensive if you get information you do not like. This will only make the other person defensive too.

○ Use what you hear as information for problem solving, not for arguing.

○ If there are differing views of something, avoid arguing about whose view is "right." Look for ways to use the differences to make positive change in the future.

○ Ask questions to give you a better understanding of the others' views and to keep the communication lines open.

○ Keep your purpose in mind – to develop your business, your staff and yourself.

○ Affirm your own intentions and the positive intentions of your staff person.

> *Keep in mind – your desired outcomes are to develop your business, your staff and yourself.*

SENDING CLEAR MESSAGES

When you are giving staff instructions, assigning work or communicating your expectations, you want to be as clear as you possibly can. While there are tips for being clear, by now you know that being clear is not a one-shot deal. It involves dialogue. An important part of sending clear messages is being willing and skilled at finding out what others have interpreted from what you have said.

What else is involved in sending clear messages?

○ **Stating the "why" of your message.**

How often have you understood every word of someone's story but not known why they were telling it? The "why" is the essential ingredient of developing independent staff who know how to do things the way you want them done. It is as important to show staff why you want your goods displayed a specific way, as it is to explain how you want it done: "I want it done this way because...."

○ **Watching the nonverbal cues and responding to them**

Does the person look like he or she is listening and following what you are saying. Does the person look confused, frustrated, or bored? When you see someone's facial expressions change, it might be a signal to do one or all of the following:

○ pick up or slow down the pace

○ ask the person for feedback

I'm not sure if I am explaining myself clearly. Can you tell me what you heard so far so I can fill in the gaps?

○ **Using more than words**

Demonstrate what you want. Show pictures and samples of what you want.

○ **Using language that states in very specific terms what you want.**

Asking staff to keep the store "neat and tidy" is not a clear request! Ask any teenager and parent for a definition of "neat and tidy" and you are likely to find very different standards.

What specifically do you mean when you say "neat and tidy". Often, in retail, housekeeping expectations are made clear through guidelines. Guidelines might state standards regarding how often window washing, dusting and vacuuming are to be done, what condition the store is to be left in at the end of the day and so on.

○ One retailer created a list of "Want To See" and "Don't Want To See" as her way of specifying clear housekeeping expectations.

One area of sending clear messages deserves special attention. That is, setting clear expectations for your staff.

COMMUNICATING CLEAR PERFORMANCE EXPECTATIONS

Staff will be more effective when they know specifically what is expected of them. Some store managers are too vague; they say they expect "good attendance", "appropriate dress" and "someone who can work well with others." These words mean different things to different people. They can lead to confusion and inconsistency.

What is good attendance? No absences? Away no more than once a month? Once every 3 months? And is an absence defined as a whole day, or partial day?

What is appropriate dress? What does this mean in terms of shoes? Jewellery? Are jeans considered appropriate? What about if they are neatly pressed? And what about hair length? How long is too long?

If you do not say what you mean, staff will assume their definitions are correct and then be surprised when you question what they are doing.

In *Achieving Customer Loyalty* (1996)[1], Marilyn Currie quotes from research reported by Ron Zemke and Chip Bell[2] (two well-known experts in the field of customer service) emphasized the value of clear expectations for creating outstanding customer service.

> *If you do not have a definition of what good service means, your chances of getting high marks from your customers is about 30%.*

> *If you have a general definition, your chances of getting high marks from your customers improve to about 50/50.*

> *If you have a detailed definition of what good service means – if it is defined in terms of both your store and the customer, if it is well communicated to employees and tied to clear forms of measurement, your chances of getting high marks from your customers are close to 90%.*

Stating what you expect can be done in two ways:

○ State the Results You Expect

○ State the Behaviours You Expect

State the Results You Want

Results are referred to by different names – outcomes, goals, objectives, targets, objectives. Let's call them goals or targets.

What results do you want in terms of gross margins, sales, customer service, displays? Sales targets can be established for each hour, shift, week or month. They may reflect dollar sales, items per sale, repeat business, etc. Just as targets can be set for sales, they can also be set for customer service, administration, visual displays and almost any activity.

Apply the idea of clear results to the role of the manager and you might consider targets like:

○ store sales of so many dollars

○ specific profit figures

○ zero staff turnover

○ high ratings by staff on the amount of coaching provided.

What would you define as clear, challenging but worthy and achievable expectations for yourself over the next month?

It's a funny thing about life; if you refuse to accept anything but the very best, you often get it!

Somerset Maughan

We know from research on motivation that goals are powerful motivators. In fact, goals or targets that are **possible but difficult** are more attractive for people and sustain their interest and effort longer than easy goals. For goals to be motivating, they must be: clear, challenging, personally meaningful, measurable and monitored.

State the Behaviour You Expect

Some results take a long time to achieve (e.g. year end profit, the success of the new line). Rather than wait, managers identify a few key behaviours that they think are essential to the end result and they develop standards (sometimes called "guidelines") that staff are expected to meet. For example, a few of the many standards for customer service might be:

- answer the phone within three rings

- acknowledge the customer within one minute

- ensure the cash out line has no more than one person waiting.

Each one of the above is clear. Staff know what is expected.

DEVELOPING COMMUNICATION EXPERTISE TAKES TIME AND PRACTICE.

Expanding your communication skills is somewhat different from knowing the facts about new merchandise. Your communication style is made up of habits and reflex actions which take practice to expand and change. Learning facts like features and benefits takes less time than learning to apply communication skills.

When you first try out new skills, you may feel a little awkward. However, this is normal. Initial clumsiness and self-consciousness will be replaced by confident, almost automatic implementation.

To practice your feedback skills, try four to five "practice" times.

- Think about a movie – describe specifically what you liked or disliked in terms of what you saw and heard and the meaning or impact it had on you.

- Think about a restaurant – describe specifically what you like or dislike in terms of what you see, hear, smell and taste and the meaning or impact on you.

- Do the same for a particular power tool – its features and benefits are very similar to other tools so be sure to be specific and descriptive.

- Think of someone you observed today. Describe specifically what you liked and disliked about the behaviour and its impact on you.

Clear expectations focus effort. Clear expectations support success.

Give copies of this chapter of the book to your staff. Teach them how to give feedback to you and to each other. Provide samples, like the ones below, and ask which ones provide the best information for learning and problem solving. Here are some starters:

FUZZY & VAGUE	MORE CLEAR AND MORE SPECIFIC
Good customer call.	*The end, where you thanked the customer for her time and for shopping with us last week – I thought that was a double compliment to her ... nice way to finish the call.*
The paperwork isn't right.	*You forgot to add the shipping charges. So we lost $....*
You're too aggressive. People here don't like working with you.	*When you raise your voice like you did just now, I think you just want to make your point. When you repeat your points as you did just now, I think you aren't interested in even considering mine. Then I get impatient and don't know what to do.*
He's unfair.	*When he lets Myra come in late as he has for the last three days, and lets Mark take longer lunches like yesterday and today, I'm upset because he is treating us all differently and it's not fair.*
I'm glad we're here so I can go over progress to date. You have all done a terrific job and the store is breaking even.	*I'm glad we're all here together so I can give you some feedback. The promotion has gone well. We made targets. Special thanks to Chris and Sam who have gone over the store average. The store is breaking even.*

The team that practices together wins!

This chapter has described several routes to clear communications. It doesn't depend solely on the words of the sender. It depends on the quality of the dialogue between people who try to understand each other.

Giving feedback and asking for it provides essential information not only for developing staff but also for improving systems and operations. Using these skills lays the groundwork for the kind of honest, clear communication that ultimately affects the bottom line. Using these skills reinforces the relationship between you and your staff as allies in building your business.

When you combine your skill in asking questions with your skill in giving feedback you teach your staff how to link their actions to their goals. You teach them to notice their impact and relate it to what they wanted to achieve. This kind of thinking leads to an interest in continuous improvement.

Teach your staff these skills as a strategy to help all of you learn together.

ACTION PLANNING

What communication ideas would you like to remember?_____

_____

_____

_____

_____

_____

What communication skills would enhance your effectiveness?_____

_____

_____

_____

_____

_____

It takes practise to develop new skills. If you are like other people, you probably need reminders to practise.

○ Put a reminder (like your response to #1 and #2 above) in your car or on your desk.

○ Write in red on your daily calendar – LISTEN or GIVE GOOD FEEDBACK.

○ Set your watch alarm for 10 a.m. and practise right after it goes off.

○ Invite your staff to help you.

[1] Currie, Marilyn. 1996. *Achieving Customer Loyalty.* Toronto: The Retail Learning Initiative.

[2] Zemke, Ron and Chip Bell. 1989. *Service Wisdom: Creating and Maintaining the Customer Service Edge.* Minneapolis: Maclean-Hunter Publishing, Lakewood Books.

Panning for Gold – Finding the Right Staff

This chapter will:

✓ show you the two different parts to recruiting staff

✓ describe six tools for identifying staffing needs

✓ help you decide what type of staff you are looking for

✓ explain what good applicants look for in making their decision

✓ provide advice from retailers on where to look for potential applicants and what to do when you find them

ATTRACTING THE RIGHT STAFF TO YOUR STORE

Please rate each of the statements below using the following scale.

1 point = Not like our store.
2 points = Somewhat like our store.
3 points = Very much like our store.

_____ 1. We take the business of finding new staff seriously.

_____ 2. Before recruiting, we review who our customers are, what types of people are currently on staff and the store needs.

_____ 3. We have a file of résumés or job applications to draw on when we need a new staff person.

_____ 4. We are aware of patterns that are changing in the kinds of customers we serve.

_____ 5. The staff reflects the various kinds of people we serve.

_____ 6. We use a staff profile to decide whom we need and when we need them to come to work.

_____ 7. I involve staff in the process of determining the specific responsibilities in the job that needs to be filled.

_____ 8. I encourage staff to let acquaintances know when we need to hire someone.

_____ 9. I make sure we are clear about job duties and responsibilities before we go looking for new staff.

_____ 10. I like to have people on staff who have different skills from mine.

_____ 11. I look for new staff members who reflect the values and beliefs that have built our business.

_____ 12. Customers and visitors think that our store would be a good place to work.

_____ **TOTAL SCORE**

Interpretation:

12 – 19   You are missing key actions that support retailers in attracting and keeping new staff.

20 – 28   You are already doing some good things. This chapter will give you some more ideas.

29 – 36   Excellent things are happening here! You'll be encouraged by what you read in this chapter.

BUILDING A TALENT BANK

Your attempts to get the right people to work in your store can be much like panning for gold. You need to know where to look. If you pan in the right place, and if you use the right tools, you may get lucky and find gold right away: or, you may need to be persistent and sift through many candidates before you find the right person. And that right person is like a gold nugget. He or she can be worth a fortune in the contribution they make to your store.

To get the right staff, you need to have lots of choice. Most of the retailers we interviewed have a file folder full of résumés of good candidates that are available for employment. Just like a prospector panning for gold, you will want to sift through a variety of possible candidates before finding the right person.

How do successful retailers get so many applicants to choose from? They create an environment that people flock to – both customers and staff! The environment they create includes the merchandise, colours, fixtures, and lighting. They hire the best people to bring the four walls and shopping experience to life. It's people that make the magic in retail.

These successful retailers' beliefs become the self-fulfilling prophecies that make their recruiting successful:

○ *We believe we are the "employer of choice." This is a great meeting place, people have fun here and everyone wants to work here.*

○ *We believe that everyone who loves books has a secret dream of working in a bookstore.*

○ *We believe that our products are the best anywhere. Everyone wants to sell our products.*

○ *We believe people have to be really good to get a job here.*

Retail offers some of the most promising career opportunities today. By the year 2000, half the population will be in service-oriented and information-related jobs! The winners will be retailers who position their jobs as career opportunities for employees, offering an orderly progression of interesting and challenging work.

RECRUITMENT HAS TWO PARTS

First, you need to know the type of person you are looking for. When people want to find out about the job before applying for it, you will be able to answer their questions. You will also need to know what you are looking for, in order to screen applicants, interview, and select the right person.

Second, you need to know how to attract potential staff.

This chapter deals with both of these areas.

IDENTIFYING YOUR STORE NEEDS

The process of finding people who might be "the right people" for your store begins long before you review résumés or application forms. It starts with some careful thinking about:

1. Your Staff
2. Your Customers
3. Your Store
4. The Job to be Done

Here are some tools you can use to think about the needs of your store before recruiting.

Tool #1 The Staff Profile

A staff profile displays a picture of all of your staff in terms of age, background, interests, experience, skills and availability for work. This profile is used, along with a customer profile, and a profile of store needs as a guide for recruitment.

Use the staff profile chart on page 15 to get a picture of your current staff.

Stephen Covey, author of *Seven Habits of Highly Effective People,* reminds us that the biggest mistake entrepreneurs make is trying to find someone who is like themselves. Retailers need to build a complementary team of people around them. Think of yourself as a band leader. For a successful sound, you need a variety of instruments. As a manager, you want variety in your staff to ensure that the store has:

- people with whom different customers can relate
- the skills required to handle a range of duties
- availability to cover every shift
- a variety of personality types (e.g. serious and fun-loving) to complement one another in their work styles.

People feel most comfortable when they can relate to the people who are selling to them. One person may feel more comfortable getting advice from a woman salesperson in a hardware store; someone else might prefer advice from a man; and others won't care as long as the person is pleasant and knowledgeable. Maximize your options by hiring men and women with different interests and backgrounds.

Tool #2 The Customer Profile

Next, consider your current and desired customer base.

Our communities and customers are changing! Many Canadian communities have become homes for a broad range of language and cultural groups. Your store needs to reflect the community it serves; a broad range of people in your staff will complement the customers and may draw additional ones!

People are changing! New interests, new roles and responsibilities mean that a different group of people may be interested in your products and services. Think of the shift in customers to do-it-yourself stores. If you want to attract people from different age, cultural or economic groups, hire staff who can relate to these customers who will help you understand the needs and expectations of this potential market.

Developing a Customer Profile, such as the one on page 87, will give you a breakdown of your current and desired customers. It will show you the estimated percentage of your customers by age group, stage in life (e.g. at school, building a career, raising a family, active in sports), background, and income level.

There are two ways to develop a Customer Profile:

○ give your best estimate of the mix of people who shop in your store and ask your staff for their perceptions

○ do some research by collecting information from your customers.

Many retailers find that developing a customer profile has the following benefits:

○ The information supports better buying and merchandising decisions.

○ You can compare the staff profile to the customer profile, and see if they match.

○ Curiosity about the accuracy of the profile encourages staff to observe the customers.

○ What you and your staff do not know about your customers becomes a source of friendly questions for staff to ask.

○ Selecting the "right person" for the job is done with a heightened awareness of the customer.

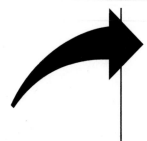

Tool #3 The Store Profile

Now that you know your staff and customer profiles, it is time to look at a profile of your store needs. The Store Profile at the end of the chapter will have to be modified to suit your store. It will help you compare what is needed with what you have available in terms of covering the hours that the store is open. It can be used to plan next week, next month or next season. In addition to filling out the chart, the following questions will help you determine store needs:

○ Does the store need staff for special tasks, e.g. receiving shipments, stocking shelves, markdowns, window displays?

○ Do you need staff who can be available "on call" with short notice, for emergencies or special events?

○ What are the responsibilities that are hardest to fill?

○ What work is seen as least desirable by the current staff?

○ How many people do you need to carry keys?

○ What are the essential qualities the store needs to balance the staff mix?

A store profile also describes the store image and product mix. You want to hire staff who reflect what the store sells in terms of image and lifestyle.

Tool #4 Job Descriptions

Can you imagine the following exchange?

Customer: *I want to buy a tool.*

Salesperson: *What kind of tool do you need, sir?*

Customer: *I haven't really thought about it. I have some really good ones at home, but I really need one or two more. What would you suggest?*

The conversation is hard to believe yet many store managers approach hiring in this way. We usually define tools according to the job we expect them to do. You should do the same when hiring people. Be clear about what you need before you go shopping. Job descriptions are important when hiring new staff.

Why Write a Job Description?

A clear job description will:

○ identify the specific knowledge, skills or experience that a candidate should have

○ help screen people who don't want this kind of work

○ give you suggestions about what to look for on an application form or résumé

○ guide you in planning and conducting a hiring interview.

What is a Job Description?

A job description clearly and concisely outlines what is involved in a job. It is usually written on one page, and states:

1. what the person is expected to do (e.g. main responsibilities and activities)

2. when (e.g. days and hours of work)

3. required skills (e.g. selling, stocking shelves, dealing with clients)

4. required qualities (e.g. friendliness, wanting to be helpful)

5. required knowledge (e.g. use a particular cash out system, customer service)

6. required qualifications (e.g. six months hardware experience)

Writing a Job Description

Writing a job description involves providing information on the six categories above. Many retailers ask their staff to review and flesh out the description. Not only do they know the job, but by asking the staff to help, you will give them an opportunity to consider new ways to structure the work. They may suggest ways to improve efficiency and effectiveness by changing the assignment of responsibilities. The opportunity to design a new job description must **not** be used as an excuse to make a list of all the undesirable tasks and lump them into one job!

Pages 89–92 contain several job descriptions that will help you get started.

Tool #5 Recruitment Planner

Based on the thinking and analysis you have done of your current staff profile, your customer profile and your store needs, you are ready to answer the key questions regarding whom you need to hire NOW. This Planner summarizes the skills, knowledge and specific experience required to fill the current vacancy. A sample appears on page 93.

It's a Two-Way Street: Would Someone Want to Work For You?

Let's assume for a moment that you know exactly what you are looking for in a new staff member. Let's also assume that you have people expressing a general interest in the job. As they move closer and find out more, will they become more excited about working in your store or will they change their minds and decide not to apply? Your recruitment efforts can be supported or sabotaged by the conditions they experience in your store.

Here are eight of the top things new staff look for. How does your store measure up?

- ○ Clean, bright, attractive place to work
- ○ Friendly, welcoming environment
- ○ Products or merchandise they like
- ○ Safety and security
- ○ Opportunity for interesting, challenging work
- ○ Opportunity to learn and grow
- ○ Competitive salary and benefits
- ○ A "good boss".

Don't underestimate the last item. More staff leave jobs because they don't like their boss than for any other reason. Fairness, consistency, respect, trust, and consistent demonstration of the values you hold dear are all powerful attractions for new and current staff.

Don't underestimate the grapevine or the "vibes" people pick up in the store. One of the powerful things about this list is that many of the things that attract good staff are also attractions to your customers. Make your store attractive to customers and it will be attractive to staff and vice versa.

Tool #6 Application Form

The next section of this chapter will identify ten ways to find candidates. Be ready for them when they come. Have an application form available.

Often "would be" staff bring in a résumé describing their experience. You may still want to ask them to fill in an application form so that all your applicants answer the same questions. If they fill it in at the store, this gives you an opportunity to notice their handwriting, ability to fill in forms and speed.

There are several sources of application forms.

- ○ You could design your own.
- ○ You could adapt one from another store.
- ○ You could buy "generic" application forms from an office supply store.

Most applications ask for the same basic kinds of information.

- ○ Name, address and telephone number
- ○ Previous work experience
- ○ Education and qualifications
- ○ References (past employers or others who know the applicant well).

The Human Rights Code

If you design your own application form, be aware that there are certain questions that should not be included. In Canada, it is against the law to consider factors such as age, race, religion, gender, and marital status when hiring (with some reasonable exceptions). Having these questions on an application form could imply that they will be used as the basis for selection, so it is better to avoid them. For more information on Human Rights provisions in hiring or legal limitations in your business, contact your retail association.

HOW TO ATTRACT GOOD APPLICANTS

Retailers say you can find gold in the following ways:

1. Keep a File of Applicants

Every single retailer we interviewed had a file of applications which they added to or subtracted from on a regular basis. Walk-ins, referrals, whatever the source, the file contained current, interested, already-interviewed applicants ready to be hired when needed. Many retailers told us that they make some initial contact with the person so they can determine if they have any interest in further discussion. If not, the résumé is not put into their file.

+ you always have possible candidates to interview or hire

+ reduces your time to search for applicants

- you have to clean the file periodically of old résumés.

2. Be Receptive to Walk-Ins

"Walk-ins" are people who come to your store because someone told them about it, or they saw a sign in the window or a mall bulletin board, or they were passing by and were curious. They could be customers, suppliers or referrals from customers or suppliers.

Most retailers find this source of people very valuable. The manager spends a few minutes talking with them, or calls them. The investment of time to screen possible candidates immediately is worthwhile.

+ most frequently used strategy of retailers

- requires screening to determine interest.

Pros (+) and Cons (-)

Word of mouth advertising is the very best.

3. Put a Sign in the Window

Signs in the window are best if they are creative: "We are looking for staff that have a great smile, love children and know about children's books"; "We are looking for coffee lovers." Take the sign out of the window after about a week to avoid having customers think you have problems attracting and keeping staff. If you still need applicants, change the sign in some way and replace the sign after some time has passed. One retailer put a small notice on a mall bulletin board where a store was to open and received over 50 résumés.

+ inexpensive, easy to install

− takes time and thought.

4. Consider Friends of Staff

These applicants may telephone, send a résumé, or walk in because they know something about the job opening or the store.

Many retailers have had excellent results with staff referring friends. "Good people refer good people" is their motto. Some retailers pay staff a referral bonus when the referred employee has completed the three month probation. One retailer will refer good candidates that she can't hire to one of the other stores in their company.

Some retailers are concerned about the friendship getting in the way of the work. It really depends on the tone and standards set and how you manage each situation.

+ staff can act as a reference and help with training

+ candidates know something about the store

− friendship may interfere with productivity

− candidate may be too much like current staff person and not add new qualities to the staff team.

5. Be a Talent Scout

This technique involves always being on the lookout for great staff. You may find potential candidates when:

○ a customer exhibits the kind of friendly nature and knowledgeable approach that you value in a staff person

○ you receive excellent service in a restaurant

○ you are shopping and the sales person goes an extra mile to help you

○ you hear friends talk about their son or daughter who is a buyer in an unrelated product and is looking for a change in focus.

Consider recruiting new talent including persons with disabilities, who would have been dismissed as possible employees just a few years ago because they wore a hearing aid or were in a wheelchair or had some other form of disability.

Once again, word of mouth marketing is the very best kind.

When you find someone with potential, approach the person and open the conversation. Explain that you manage a retail store and are always interested in meeting people who demonstrate the kind of values and skills that you want in your store. Give the person your business card. Tell them if they are ever interested, or if anyone like them is ever interested in talking about an opportunity in retail, to please give you a call or drop by the store. A bonus could be that the person could become a customer!

"Talent scout" recruiting gets mixed reviews. Some retailers frown on recruiting from the competition on principle: "Do unto others as you would have them do unto you." Others say: "Presenting someone with an idea to consider is not robbing the competition, because people are exposed to opportunities all the time through newspapers and friends." Some retailers reported that they will not recruit from the competition within their own mall or on their street, but will talk with excellent staff outside their geographic area. They would not recruit on the premises but would request an opportunity to meet and talk at a later date.

+ you can attract experienced people whom you have seen in action

+ people love to be complimented on doing a good job

- some retailers are uncomfortable with approaching the competition

- the other retailer might retaliate by recruiting your staff.

6. Use Classified Advertising

Placing ads in local newspapers is another way to find applicants. This is an effective way to find managers, department heads, buyers, etc. It also works well for a new store opening when you are hiring a number of people. The ad needs to be well-written and clear about your requirements and expectations.

One retailer ran a local ad, interviewed 250 people and hired 16. He wanted to hire the best available and would not compromise. He was prepared to go the extra mile to ensure he got the best. Store reports indicate his staff are outstanding in customer friendliness and speed of service. When people realize that you will not settle for less than the best, your reputation for having high standards will become known in the community.

+ a way to do two things at once: give your store visibility and attract applicants

+ requires a well-organized screening process

+ may get several staff from one ad

- it costs money

- requires very thorough screening and interviewing

- can be a time-consuming process to respond to applicants and enquiries

- image can be affected by not responding in a timely way to applicants.

7. Place Notices on Bulletin Boards

Bulletin boards in local high schools, colleges and universities work for finding both full-time and part-time staff. A phone call to the school, then dropping off your notice is generally all that is required. Interested applicants will drop in to see you in the store. Retailers report that one sign brings many résumés to screen and people to interview. This strategy is also effective when you want to fill many positions, for example, for the Christmas season.

This is an effective strategy to let people who are starting retail careers know about the opportunity in your store. Most community colleges offer courses in marketing and management. Some offer courses on assortment planning and buying in fashion, which can be applied to many types of products.

+ no cost and lots of potential returns

+ people are local and can get to work easily

- you may be inundated with dozens of résumés.

8. Recruit at Career Days –
Through Colleges, Schools or Placement Firms

In this approach, someone from your company would participate in the career day and interview interested applicants at their site. Job specifications would have been posted in advance so that students could book time for interviews.

Court many, wed few

This approach was recommended by retailers who were looking for graduates from a retailing or marketing program with the intention of grooming them for long-term careers in their businesses. These retailers offered store staff the opportunity to do the preliminary interviews.

+ attract people who are well-educated and interested in retail

+ may be able to hire several staff with one visit

+ low cost

- requires planning, lead time for the process, intense schedule of interviews.

9. Consider a Member of Your Own Family

Family members as a source of new staff got mixed reports. Some retailers believe in it because they respect, trust, and can depend on family members. They report harmony in the store because staff accept the situation. Other retailers will hire family members only if each one would be working in a different location, e.g. a different store in the chain. Others will not allow staff to manage a family member. The main concerns seem to be security and working relationships. This is a choice you have to make.

+ family members tend to be loyal to each other

- family relationships can interfere with business relationships

- other staff may be uncomfortable and feel there is favouritism.

10. Grow Your Own Staff

"Grow your own staff" is a philosophy of many successful retailers. They focus on hiring part-timers, teach them and promote them to full-time, teach them some more and promote them to assistant managers, teach them more and promote them to store managers. In one company, a store manager with outstanding sales skills is being promoted to be the training manager so she can teach everyone else how to sell as well as she does.

The key here is to provide challenges, support and opportunity to the staff you value and want to keep. Their growth is a key factor in your ability to "grow" your business.

WHY IT'S WORTH IT TO BUILD A BANK OF TALENTED APPLICANTS

When a staff member resigns, you usually don't get much notice.

If you have applicants waiting to be interviewed or waiting to be hired, it makes your life easier. With some concentrated effort you can hire a new staff person within a few days. If you have to start from scratch looking for applicants, life will be more difficult. First, the open position puts pressure on your existing staff. Second, as the manager you will feel pressure to focus on recruiting and may let other things slide. This puts pressure on you. The longer the search for the right person goes on, the greater the likelihood that you will compromise your standards and settle for someone less than ideal for the position. It's human nature, and it is not good for business.

THE LESSON: KEEP YOUR FILES FULL OF APPLICATIONS!

You should be recruiting all the time! Keep your eyes and ears open for potential candidates so that when you need to hire, you will have a talent bank from which to hire the best.

STAFF PROFILE

Write the name of each staff person in a separate box across the top of the chart below.

Staff Names →							
Male							
Female							
Teenager (below 20)							
Young adult (20-35)							
Early middle age (36-50)							
Middle age adult (51-65)							
Older age adult (65+)							
Visible minority							
Interests/hobbies (write in)							
Years experience: In retail:							
In your store:							
Can come in on short notice (Yes/No)							
Available Monday							
Available Tuesday							
Available Wednesday							
Available Thursday							
Available Friday							
Available Saturday							
Available Sunday							
Reflects store image							
Reflects the customer profile							
Relates well to customers even though does not visibly reflect customers							

CUSTOMER PROFILE

GROUP	SPECIFIC DETAILS	% TODAY	% IN 3 YRS.
Women	*20-39 yrs. mostly with young children*	*15 %*	*10 %*
	40-59 yrs. mostly working	*50*	*35*
	60-79 yrs. with grandchildren	*30*	*50*
Other		*5*	*5*

○ Women
- ○ Teenagers
- ○ Young Adults (20-35)
- ○ Early Middle Years (36 – 50)
- ○ Middle Age (51 – 65)
- ○ Older Age (65 plus)

○ Men
- ○ Teenagers
- ○ Young Adults (20-35)
- ○ Early Middle Years (36 – 50)
- ○ Middle Age (51 – 65)
- ○ Older Age (65 plus)

○ Leisure Interests
- ○ Watching Sports
- ○ Playing Sports
- ○ Reading
- ○ Building Things
- ○ Theatre
- ○ Music
- ○ Movies
- ○ Volunteer Work

○ Income Level

STORE PROFILE

TIME FRAME	☐ Now		☐ Next Month		☐ Next Season		
	Mon.	Tues.	Wed.	Thurs.	Fri.	Sat.	Sun.
opening time							
closing time							
peak hours							
# of staff needed							
# of staff available							
slow hours							
# of staff needed							
# of staff available							
Shift 1 Time							
# of staff needed							
# of staff available							
Shift 2 Time							
# of staff needed							
# of staff available							
Shift 3 Time							
# of staff needed							
# of staff available							
Available staff relate well to customers -If no, what is needed?							
Available staff reflect store image -If no, what is needed?							

SAMPLE JOB DESCRIPTION

Title: STORE MANAGER

PRIMARY FUNCTION

As a store manager, you will ensure that the store is professionally staffed. You are directly responsible for the performance of each staff person in your store. You are expected to maintain a high level of professionalism, so as to provide a model for your staff. You are required to provide coaching and training to assist your staff in reaching their sales goals. As manager, you are responsible for the security of store assets and the achievement of store performance goals.

Job Duties/Expectations

Sales Management

- ○ ensure that sales and service goals are met
- ○ track daily actual sales vs. projected sales
- ○ set individual sales goals for staff

Customer Service

- ○ develop customer service policies and ensure they are implemented
- ○ develop a customer base through use of preferred customer lists
- ○ develop a system to recognize customer service excellence

Staff Training

- ○ ensure all new staff are properly oriented to the company
- ○ coach staff to improve their skills
- ○ ensure that there are ongoing training sessions to develop staff
- ○ convene and lead effective staff meetings on a regular basis
- ○ train staff in store operations

Scheduling

- ○ understand store traffic patterns and schedule accordingly
- ○ involve staff in scheduling process

Administration

- ○ understand the POS terminal and procedures related to purchases
- ○ ensure cash reports and deposits are balanced daily
- ○ develop effective systems for loss prevention and monitor them
- ○ develop a procedure to track staff discounts and clothing allowances

Title: STORE MANAGER continued

Staff Management

- ○ treat all staff with respect
- ○ use knowledge of motivation to stimulate excitement
- ○ provide positive reinforcement on a regular basis
- ○ review sales and service performance weekly

Hiring

- ○ comply with company policy regarding selection procedures and reference checks
- ○ ensure there are applications on file

Merchandise

- ○ manage inventory levels to maximize profit
- ○ ensure window displays are changed every two weeks
- ○ ensure the store is merchandised to advantage
- ○ develop and implement procedures to track damaged or returned stock
- ○ ensure markdowns are handled in a timely and accurate way

Store Upkeep

- ○ ensure housekeeping standards are developed and maintained
- ○ ensure a thorough cleaning of the entire store is done once a year

Job Requirements

Skills: management, selling, customer relations, buying, merchandising, coaching and training

Qualities: integrity, fairness, sense of humour

Knowledge: products, POS system, suppliers

Qualifications: minimum two years experience

SAMPLE JOB DESCRIPTION
Title: SALES STAFF

PRIMARY FUNCTION

To help customers buy our products. To generate sales and provide customer service and satisfaction. To perform a variety of tasks that support sales and service (e.g. merchandising, housekeeping, restocking, etc.).

Job Duties/Expectations

Help Customers Buy Our Products

- ⭕ communicate product knowledge to the customer as appropriate
- ⭕ assist customer in locating and trying on merchandise
- ⭕ suggest add-on products to meet customer needs

Generate Sales

- ⭕ ensure customers are greeted within 60 seconds
- ⭕ determine customer needs
- ⭕ close the sale in a professional and timely manner

Develop Customer Base

- ⭕ explain preferred customer program
- ⭕ record repeat customer preferences and follow up as new merchandise arrives

Contribute to the Store Climate through Teamwork

- ⭕ maintain positive communication habits
- ⭕ work co-operatively to maintain a team spirit

Support Sales and Service

- ⭕ carry out procedures and maintain standards in the following areas: loss prevention, merchandise handling and presentation, housekeeping, restocking, cashing out
- ⭕ maintain data integrity in all systems
- ⭕ other duties as requested

Personal Development

- ⭕ ensure product knowledge is up-to-date
- ⭕ continue to develop professional skill and knowledge base

Note: The research for this book indicates that there are considerable differences among retailers regarding their requirements for skills, qualities, knowledge and qualifications. Therefore these aspects of a job description have not been included.

SAMPLE JOB DESCRIPTION
Title: PART-TIME CASHIER

(This position applies to all staff who traditionally work evenings or weekends, with hours that fluctuate from week to week.)

POSITION SUMMARY:

This position not only entails cash duties but also shelving, helping customers, maintaining the store in a neat and tidy appearance.

Job Duties and Responsibilities:

- ring in all sales
- cash out sales at the end of the day or shift
- help customers on the phone or in the store
- keep the store tidy, cleaning the store at the end of the shift
- straighten shelves and cash desk
- make sure windows are neat and presentable
- follow proper procedures regarding returns and refunds
- complete the receiving paper work, if required

Job Requirements:

(varied from retailer to retailer)

SAMPLE JOB DESCRIPTION
Title: BACK ROOM STAFF PERSON

DUTIES:

- responsible for receiving all merchandise, entering paperwork into the system, and unpacking and warehousing the merchandise
- ensure that all shelves are properly stocked
- co-ordinate the returns including distribution of returns list
- ensure all displays are clean, neat, and changed regularly
- ensure all reports are accurate and complete
- ensure all outgoing orders are accurate, complete and on time
- co-ordinate all special orders and contact customers
- ensure the bulletin board is up-to-date with pertinent information

RECRUITMENT PLANNER

1. **When do you need staff for?**

Days	M	T	W	T	F	S	S
Hours	___	___	___	___	___	___	___
Number of Part-time	☐	☐	☐	☐	☐	☐	☐
Number of Full-time	☐	☐	☐	☐	☐	☐	☐

2. **What skills do you need? Consider staff profile, store profile and job description.**

3. **What types of people do you need? Consider customer profile and staff profile.**

Hiring The Best

This chapter will:

✓ take you through nine stages involved in selecting and hiring new staff

✓ provide tips on screening applicants, planning and conducting interviews, checking references and making a job offer

✓ show you how to ask the types of questions that will help you find out what the candidate has done, can do, wants to do and will do

✓ introduce probing techniques to draw out information during an interview

✓ recommend doing a second interview and provide suggestions

✓ list common pitfalls in interviewing

✓ help you make your offer attractive

HIRING THE BEST!

Use the following scale to assess how you hire new staff.

1 point = Not all like me.   **2 points = Somewhat like me.**   **3 points = Very much like me.**

____1.   I think past performance is a very important consideration when making a hiring decision.

____2.   I read résumés and application forms carefully.

____3.   A pre-interview telephone call or short face-to-face chat provides a preliminary screening of candidates.

____4.   I plan my interview questions in advance so that I find out what the candidate has done (past experience), can do (current experience), and will do (availability and willingness).

____5.   I use a list of desirable characteristics to rate applicants.

____6.   I allow sufficient time for an in-depth interview.

____7.   I try to make the candidate comfortable during the interview.

____8.   I keep notes to remind me of what was said during the interview.

____9.   I get specific, detailed information from the candidate during the interview.

____10. I give detailed information about the job responsibilities to the candidate.

____11. I inform candidates of the date when they will hear from me.

____12. I check references supplied by the candidate.

____13. I am careful to use questions that respect human rights.

____14. I interview a second time.

____15. If I am unsure of which person to hire, I give myself time to think about it.

____16. I personally notify everyone that is interviewed about our final decision.

____17. Once we have offered someone a job, I stay in regular contact until the person is "on board."

____18. I make sure that everyone interviewed leaves with a positive impression of our store.

____   **TOTAL SCORE**

Interpretation:

18 – 24   If you are hiring additional people, use this chapter as a guide.

25 – 34   This chapter will give you many ideas to use in your hiring process.

35 – 44   You do lots of good things in your hiring process. You'll be encouraged by what you read in this chapter.

45 – 54   You have excellent hiring practices already!

TOOLS FOR SELECTING NEW STAFF

The Best Predictors of Success!

If you could consider only one thing when deciding whether someone would be an effective staff person in your store, what would it be? Her smile, enthusiasm, love of the product? A great deal of research in the area of selection has dealt with this question and the answer is always the same.

The best predictor of what someone will do is what the person has done in the past!

If there is no past work history, consider experience in volunteer jobs or personal interest areas that relate to your business. If there are no suitable candidates available, take a chance on a person who does not have any related experience. We all got our first job this way.

Several retailers we spoke to are not concerned about sales skills or retail experience. They look at past performance to learn about attitudes toward people and work.

- ○ *We can teach them about retail, our products and how to sell. We want someone with enthusiasm to learn, a desire to help people, a friendly personality and excitement about our product.*

As a general rule, knowledge and skills are much easier to teach than values and beliefs. You can influence people's behaviour, but you can't change their personalities.

People tend to continue doing the same things they have done in the past. In other words:

- ○ If a person has been an enthusiastic and co-operative employee before, he or she will likely show the same attributes in your store.

- ○ If a person has a lengthy record of being late and absent (without specific cause), they might be late and absent in your workplace as well.

The next sections describe the stages in selecting the best person for the job opening. Considerable attention is given to questions that help you assess what candidates have done in the past, and what values and beliefs they are likely to bring to a job.

> People will repeat patterns of behaviour. Focus on what they have done!

STAGES IN HIRING THE BEST

There are nine stages to hiring the best.

1. Screen Candidates

2. Plan the Interview

3. Conduct the Interview

4. Conduct a Second Interview

5. Check References

6. Make the Decision

7. Make the Job Offer

8. Notify and Thank All Candidates

9. Support the Transition to Your Store

Stage 1 of Hiring the Best

Screen Candidates

Read the Résumé or Application Carefully

Sometimes the most important information on an application form is what it does not say! The absence of information may not rule out a candidate from consideration, but the gaps or inconsistencies should be noted and explored during a screening phone call or interview. You will want more information when you see the following:

○ gaps in employment history

○ lack of references or references where there are no phone numbers or addresses

○ the name of a fellow employee instead of the name of the supervisor or manager at a previous job

○ a blank left in the space that asks for the reason for leaving a job.

Everyone tries to make their work history, experience and qualifications look as positive and attractive as possible. In some application forms, there is a note stating: "Providing incorrect information on this application form may be grounds for dismissal." Usually, dismissal is justified only when there are outright lies about experience, qualifications, or other key information.

The Telephone Screening Call

Invest five to ten minutes to determine whether you want to spend more time interviewing the applicant. A sample call would sound like this:

○ *I am looking at your application form/résumé and I wonder if you have a few minutes to talk.*

○ *Thank you for applying for the position of buyer at the store I manage. Your résumé/application is interesting to me. I have some preliminary questions I'd like to ask you, such as: What attracts you to our store? What would be the ideal job for you now? I think it will take about 10 minutes. Is this a good time to talk? Please feel free to say "No," and I'll call you back when it is more convenient. I would like to talk to you fairly soon because the conversation will help both of us decide whether or not we should schedule an interview.*

Demonstrate the courtesy you appreciate in others.

By mentioning the questions you want to ask during your opening statement, you give the person a sense of what you want to talk about and a few seconds to think.

When the applicant is available to talk on the telephone, ask questions like:

○ *What would be the ideal job for you at this time?*

○ *What kind of work do you enjoy doing?*

○ *Why did you apply to this store? What appealed to you?*

○ *What hours will you be available for work?*

Ask other questions relating to major gaps or inconsistencies that you noticed on the résumé or application.

Toward the end of the telephone call, decide whether you want to interview the candidate or not:

I believe it would be worth it to both of us to meet and talk further. How do you feel?

OR

At this time, I don't think we have a good match between what you are looking for and what I need.

Another decision you have to make is whether to keep this person's application in your talent bank for future consideration, or not:

I will keep your application on file for future consideration. Thank you for your interest and time.

OR

I want to wish you good luck in your job search. I appreciate your interest in our store. Goodbye.

Information from Another Interviewer

Another very helpful form of pre-screening can be information from someone else who has already interviewed your candidate. You may have a colleague in another store who interviewed the person. As one retailer said:

Other stores in our chain will refer good candidates to us. Perhaps the store is not hiring right now, or the available hours won't work for the person, or it is an inconvenient location for the candidate. We value the information they pass along to us about the candidate.

Stage 2 of Hiring the Best

Plan the Job Interview

A carefully planned interview will be the key to your success. The interview must accomplish two objectives:

- ○ provide you with the information you need to make the right hiring decision
- ○ give the candidate the information he or she needs to decide whether the job is attractive.

The goal is a win-win for each of you. Both of you must be confident and enthusiastic about the decision in order for the relationship to be successful.

Managing Time

- ○ Allow a minimum of 45 minutes for an interview. Even though you may be able to do it in less, you don't want to cut the exchange short because of another commitment.

- ○ Schedule breaks for yourself between interviews. An effective interview requires a lot of concentration and energy. You need to be alert and focused.

Managing Your Memory

- ○ Plan to take notes in order to keep track of what was said. After interviewing several people, the details begin to blur and you may forget who said what. A rating sheet like the following helps to summarize your observations and the information received:

CANDIDATE RATING SHEET

NAME _____ DATE _____

FACTOR:	RATING (1 is low, 5 is high)				
Enthusiasm	1	2	3	4	5
Caring manner	1	2	3	4	5
Smile and friendly nature	1	2	3	4	5
Grooming	1	2	3	4	5
Listening skills	1	2	3	4	5
Selling skills	1	2	3	4	5
Customer service approach	1	2	3	4	5
Experience	1	2	3	4	5
etc.					

Planning Your Questions

Design your interview questions carefully. They will be the key to getting the right information for making your decision. Every important quality or characteristic that you require should be reflected in your questions. Consider the following types:

- ❍ "Have Done" questions
- ❍ "Prefer to Do" questions
- ❍ "Can Do" questions
- ❍ "Will Do" questions

Experience

"Have Done" Questions

"Have Done" questions are designed to find out about the experience and past performance of the candidate. They include questions such as:

- ○ *What were your specific duties at Givens Sporting Goods?*

- ○ *Describe how you handled a return or refund, or a customer who couldn't make up her mind.*

- ○ *What kind of differences did you find when you moved from buying accessories to buying sweaters?*

- ○ *What aspects of your education and training will help you be effective in a bookstore?*

- ○ *Have you ever taken any formal sales or customer service training courses? What can you use in this job?*

- ○ *Tell me about a time when you were faced with an upset customer. What was the problem? What did she say and what did you say? What was the outcome?*

- ○ *Describe a time when you worked with another employee on a special job or project. What did you do? How did it work out?*

It's easy to ask "Have Done" questions in relation to the jobs the candidate has listed on the application form. The answers will help you understand both the experience the candidate has had, and how they have approached the different aspects of their jobs. You will learn a lot about their values and preferences if you add "prefer to do" questions.

Desire

"Prefer To Do" Questions

- ○ *Working in retail is a lot more than just selling to customers. Tell me about some of the other things you did when you worked at Keenos Shoes. Which responsibilities did you enjoy the most? The least? Why?*

- ○ *What would you like to have a chance to do? What would you like to learn more about?*

- ○ *If you were given a choice between doing the markdowns or cleaning the store, which would you choose? Why?*

- ○ *If you could choose between coaching a sales person to deal with an indecisive customer or coaching the person to serve a customer with a complaint, which would you choose? Why?*

"Can Do" Questions

Design these questions to find out about the knowledge and skills the candidate currently has that could be relevant to the job opening. For example:

○ *I'd like to discuss how you approach different situations that come up in most retail stores. I'm wondering what questions you would ask a customer who is returning a product? A customer who is "just browsing?"*

○ *How would you handle it if the store was busy, and a parent who was looking at our merchandise did not notice that her child was pulling merchandise off the shelves?*

One of the most effective ways to assess "Can Do" is to role play. Here is how one retailer does it:

○ *I want to know if the candidate can sell, so I ask them to tell me about sales they have made in the past, how they qualify a customer, overcome objections, etc. Then, I ask them to sell me something right there on the spot. It doesn't matter whether it's the sweater they are wearing or the coffee cup on the table: "Sell me something." Then I integrate what they **told** me about how they sell with what I actually **saw** them do. Of course, I take into account the artificiality of selling to me and the pressure in it. But you'd be surprised at how much you can learn from this.*

○ *I'd like you to sell me something, anything. A book you enjoyed, a video or movie that grabbed your attention, an object in this room, anything.*

○ *I hear your reasons to buy this product but I'm still not sure I will like it later. What might you say?*

"Will Do" Questions

Design your "Will Do" questions to assess the willingness of a candidate to do the job. For example:

○ *We have regular training sessions on Saturday mornings starting at.... Will you be able to attend? How would you feel about coming in for them?*

○ *Would you be willing to work on the computerized inventory system?*

○ *Can you come in on short notice occasionally? On what days is that possible?*

○ *How do you feel about spending some part of every month unloading boxes from the delivery trucks and unpacking them?*

○ *Image of the store is important. We take pride in how the store looks. What housekeeping duties are you willing to do daily?*

○ *Are you willing to follow the dress code that we have here?*

Questions that give you an idea of what the person is like in terms of values and beliefs are best asked after other more factual questions. Some examples are:

○ *Describe your best boss to me. What was great about him or her?*

○ *Describe your favourite store to me. What makes that store your favourite?*

○ *If there was one thing you could change in your present store, what would that be?*

○ *What is the one thing that you need to learn to be even more successful? What do you need to do less of?*

○ *If I were to ask your boss to describe you to me, how would they describe you?*

○ *What would your co-workers say?*

○ *Give me an example of a situation where you had to learn the "hard way."*

○ *What kinds of things do you do in your leisure time?*

You may want to consider the following as a final question:

○ *It's hard to discuss everything in a half hour or so. Tell me, is there anything else you think I should know about you?*

Conduct Effective Interviews

Consider the following interview model. It includes four steps.

1. The Opening   Set the Tone and Build Rapport
2. Information Gathering Find Out about the Candidate
3. Information Giving   Tell the Candidate about the Job
4. The Closing   End on a Positive Note, and the Next Steps

Stage 3 of Hiring the Best

Step 1 of an Interview

The Opening – Set the Tone and Build Rapport

Interviews can be nerve-wracking events for some candidates. After all, if the person really wants (or needs) the job, there is a lot at stake! In the best of circumstances, most of us find it challenging to be in the spotlight, answering questions about ourselves to a relative stranger.

As an interviewer, it is important that you manage this tension so that it helps rather than blocks the person. Here are some suggestions to "ease into the process" in a positive, non-threatening way:

○ **Establish Rapport with the Candidate.** Make it clear that you are interested in the person.

Did you find a place to park easily? How were my directions?

○ **Welcome Them and Thank Them.**

I'm glad to meet you and really appreciate your making time for us to chat.

○ **Explain the Purpose.** Take a few minutes to review why you are meeting. It is an opportunity for both of you to find out more about each other and make a decision about whether there is a good "fit."

I want to learn about you, your hopes, experiences and preferences. And, I think you want to learn about me, the job, and our store. In our conversation we will explore these areas so that each of us can make a decision about whether this is a good "fit" for both of us. How does that sound to you?

○ **Outline the Ground Rules.** The candidate will be eager to know what is expected. Explain the kind of information you are interested in, the information you will share about the job, the approximate length of the interview, etc.

I want to learn more about the type of job you want, what your past experience has been, and how your skills and interests fit with our store, our way of doing business and the job we have open. I also want to tell you about the job and about us, and answer any questions you may have. I have set aside 45 minutes for our conversation. Is this what you were expecting? Shall I begin with some questions?

○ **Get Off to an Easy Start.** Make sure the first question is an open-ended one that will be fairly easy for the person to answer.

Why don't you begin by telling me a little about your most recent job. What kinds of things have you been doing? What did you enjoy most about that job?

Gather Information

Use the Planned Questions to Find Out about the Candidate

Once the tone and expectations for the interview have been set, it is time to get to know the candidate. Use the questions you planned to use prior to the interview. Having all the candidates answer the same questions helps you compare apples to oranges when you choose among them, after the interview.

Red Flag Areas

In some cases, you may encounter "red flag" areas that alert you to probe for more information. "Red flags" take the form of:

Incomplete information	Silence
Misunderstanding	Clarification required
Unexpected answers	Changing the subject
Avoiding certain topics	Contradictions

Some of the following techniques will help you gather information on these areas.

Ways to Draw Out Information

A probe is a communications skill designed to draw out more information. This is an important technique because it helps you avoid jumping to conclusions and making assumptions. Some successful ways of probing are described next.

See also Chapters 2 – 5 on communication.

Probing questions are always useful in communications

Expectant Silence	When you are quiet for more than three seconds, it usually indicates to the candidate that you would like to know more. *Uh huh....* Nodding your head.
Echo or Repeat	Repeat part of the candidate's last statement in the form of a question. *You were frustrated?*
Define or Clarify	Ask for a more detailed explanation of the candidate's response. *What do you mean when you say you were "passed over?"*
Summarize	Recap the person's information or feelings as a way of checking to see if you have it right. *So you didn't feel like you got the recognition you deserved when you made those three changes? Right?*
Explore Inconsistencies	Describe differences that you have heard and ask for an explanation. *Help me understand this. A moment ago you said "x." Now you are saying "y." Would you say more about this please?*

Nonverbal Behaviour

It is important to remember that non-verbal behaviour can encourage or discourage communication. Actions such as nodding, smiling, leaning forward, maintaining eye contact, and pausing will usually encourage more communication. Frowns, looking away, shaking your head, or looking at your watch will make the person "clam up." Use your non-verbal communication skills to manage the interview. Encourage an extended answer when that is appropriate and limit the conversation when required.

Give Information

Tell the Candidate about the Job

When you finish your questions, you will want to provide information to the candidate about yourself, the job and the store.

How much time you spend giving information depends on how interested you both are in working together. If you listen and read the candidate's body language, you will know if the person is not really interested in the job. If someone does not seem interested, ask what questions the person has, and respond. If you are not sure about someone's interest level, you can ask: "What is your interest level so far in the job?" If the person seems interested and you think the candidate is a good one, provide a lot of information.

What to Tell a Candidate

Describe the job in detail and begin to "sell" it as well. That means, sell the unique features of the store, the merchandise, the team and yourself. Talk about:

- ○ what makes the store special
- ○ your values and beliefs about staff and customers
- ○ the specific duties in the job
- ○ your expectations, e.g. dress code, housekeeping, ethics
- ○ salary, benefits, compensation
- ○ likely working hours or work schedule
- ○ other staff members – who they are and how they work together
- ○ the working environment – describe the store as a staff person would
- ○ your way of working as the store manager – your style.

During this part of the interview, many retailers will paint two pictures for the candidate: the rosy one and the grey one. One retailer said:

We often tell the candidate about the down side of the job as well as the up side, e.g. the late hours when a customer hangs around, the angry customers who can get you down if you let them, the missed lunches because the store is so busy. We want to see how the candidate will deal with this information. We want to be realistic with them.

A Probation Period is an Element of the Job

Most of the retailers we talked to have a probation period for new staff members, both part-time and full-time. Three months is usually considered a reasonable amount of time to assess the "fit" between the job and the new person. It is considered a transition period for both parties. The new person assesses the job, the store, comfort with the environment, the merchandise, the customers, the other staff and the manager. You assess how the new person is adapting, learning and fitting in with the store operation.

It is important to let the candidate know about the probation period during the hiring interview.

It is reassuring for them to know that during this period they will get feedback on how they are doing, and support for learning.

Ask the Candidate for Questions

You further demonstrate respect for the candidate when you say: "I have been asking you questions for awhile, now let's turn it around and give you an opportunity to fire some at me. What can I answer for you?"

You learn a lot if you listen to the type of questions that candidates ask. Usually, their questions reveal what is important to them.

Close the Interview

End on a Positive Note, and Clarify the Next Steps

Your goal should be to have all candidates feel good about themselves, good about you as the manager and good about your store. Remember:

- they might re-apply
- they will tell others about their experience
- they are potential customers.

An effective closing will include the following features:

- *next steps*
- *feedback*
- *thank you*

Next Steps

People like to know when the final decisions will be made and how they will be notified. It makes good sense to provide clear information about these matters. This is also the time to tell them that you may request a second interview.

- *I will be completing the first interviews on Friday. You can expect to receive a call from me over the weekend. If you are selected, I would like you to come back next week for a second interview.*

Feedback

People need to know what their chances are of getting the job. If you do not intend to hire them, let them down gently, but be straightforward.

- *I enjoyed learning about your background today. At this time I do not believe this opportunity will match your needs and our needs. If you get more hardware experience, I would like to talk to you again.*

- *I appreciate your interest in wanting to work here. Your availability for work is not a good fit for our needs right now. Call me if you find you can work evenings and we can talk again.*

- *I want to thank you for coming in to see us today. I must admit that your lack of retail experience in a bookstore is a big stumbling block right now. We are looking for someone who really knows our business.*

Thank You

Let them know you appreciate them and their time.

- *I enjoyed the time we spent together. Thank you for your time and interest in our store. Good luck with your job search.*

- *Thank you for spending time with me today. We don't have a fit right now, but I hope our paths cross again sometime in the future. All the best to you.*

- *You certainly impressed me with your experience and your positive and enthusiastic outlook toward selling. I want to speak with you again. Think about the position over the weekend and call me on Monday with an indication of your interest. Thanks again. It was a pleasure to talk with you.*

Treat every candidate with courtesy and respect. Whether hired or not, they will tell others how you treated them.

Be careful!

Common Interview Pitfalls

There are some common mistakes that could result in your passing up a promising candidate or hiring someone who will not be a good fit later. Avoid these pitfalls.

○ **Talking Too Much.** There is an 80/20 rule in interviewing. The interviewer should listen 80 percent of the time and speak 20 percent of the time.

○ **Giving the Candidate the Right Answer.** Be aware that questions such as the following tell the candidate what you want and potentially bias the response you will get:

You wouldn't mind working the late shift, would you? We need someone who can do window displays, you can do that, can't you? We want someone promotable. What are your career plans?

○ **Being Overly Influenced by Appearances.** Consider the "whole" person. While the way people look and talk is important in retail, probe beyond the surface to appreciate the range of talent the person could actually add to your store.

○ **Being Overly Influenced by your Biases.** One store manager was very proud of her strong-willed, assertive manner. She felt that this was such an important characteristic that all of her staff should be very strong-willed and assertive as well. The staff she assembled intimidated many customers and fought a lot among themselves.

○ **Asking Insensitive or Illegal Questions.** In the past, it may have been acceptable to say things like the following:

You're too old (young) for this job.

You're not going to quit and have a baby, are you?

We were actually looking for a woman (man).

Your accent (appearance, dress) wouldn't work here.

These questions and statements are not acceptable.

Stage 4 of Hiring the Best

Conduct a Second Interview

All the retailers in the sample for this book conduct a second interview before offering a full-time or part-time permanent job. They invest the time to see the person again on a different day under different circumstances because they know it minimizes the risk and maximizes the chance of success for the candidate, the manager and the store.

Here are some suggestions from other retailers:

○ Don't repeat the first interview. Consider a different setting, and possibly even a different (or additional) interviewer. A senior member of staff, assistant manager or someone else with an in-depth understanding of your store will add a new element and a second opinion. New questions will have come to you as you thought about the potential fit between this specific person and the job.

○ Interview the candidate near another store, even the competition, and ask them to point out the differences between the two stores.

○ Include some other activities such as touring the store, meeting several staff members, etc.

○ Focus on the most important qualities you require in a new staff member.

○ Make liberal use of "Can Do," "Will Do" and "Prefer to Do" questions.

○ Use the opportunity to "sell" the store and the job.

○ Urge the candidate to ask questions throughout the interview.

○ Let the candidate get a feel for the merchandise and ask questions.

The first interview narrows the field. The second interview enables you to make a final decision.

One retailer will bring a person back a third time to ensure she has all the information she needs to feel comfortable about making the hiring decision. You don't need to apologize to candidates for asking them to come back. You can say: "It is an important decision that we both are making and I want to be sure it is the right one for both of us."

Check References

Stage 5 of Hiring the Best

Every retailer we interviewed does reference checks. Some admitted they learned the hard way and therefore will not compromise when it comes to checking references. They conduct a minimum of two on each candidate considered for employment. At least one must be a business reference, a boss, customer or co-worker.

A reference check helps you manage the risk before making the decision. Reference checks help you:

○ confirm information about qualifications and experience

○ get information on a person's strengths and possible weaknesses.

Candidates and store staff see that the job is important when the manager makes time for more than one interview.

Stage 6 of Hiring the Best

The usual steps in a reference check are:

1. Identify yourself, your title and location.

2. Explain that you are interviewing the candidate for a specific job.

3. You are contacting former employers or people who know the candidate.

4. Establish that you are speaking to the right person to get this information.

5. Ask for their help in providing a reference.

6. Confirm the employment record.

    When did this person work for you? From when to when?

    What were his/her responsibilities?

    What kinds of things did he or she do as part of these responsibilities?

    What were the person's strengths and areas for improvement in that job?

7. Describe the current job that was applied for.

8. Ask if they would consider this candidate suitable for this kind of job.

9. Ask what words they would use to describe the candidate as an employee.

10. Find out why the person left this job.

    I'm wondering how it happened that (this person) left your company?

11. Ask if they would rehire the person.

12. Ask if there is anything else you should know or consider before making your decision about this person.

Not all organizations are willing to answer every question and not all will answer candidly. Usually you will be able to tell by what they don't say or by their tone of voice if there is some question about the person's suitability for employment. The probing techniques mentioned earlier will work in this interview as well.

Make the Decision

Hiring a staff person is a big decision that will affect your store, the life of the candidate and the morale and effectiveness of your staff. Don't make it lightly. There are times when most indicators say "Go." There will be times when a few red flags say "Caution." There will be times when you are not sure. You may need to delay. Sleep on it. If in the morning you still are unsure, say "NO."

Don't Compromise

Even though you may need to hire quickly to relieve the pressure on staff that an open position creates, don't compromise. If you hire the wrong person, the time required for coaching and training will be greater and it will not necessarily be a solution. Remember, also, the time it will take if you have to replace the person later.

Make the Job Offer

Stage 7 of Hiring the Best

Once you have made the decision, contact the selected candidate first.

Present the job offer in a positive way, as an exciting opportunity. Outline some of the reasons for your decision in terms of the skills and experience the person will bring. If possible, get a verbal commitment immediately that they are willing to accept the job offer. Let the candidate know how happy you are to have them coming "on board."

> *I'm calling to offer you the sales position with our store. Everyone you met was impressed with you and your background. Your references supported all the information you gave us. I'm excited about your becoming a member of our team. Silence – while you listen to their response. I am very pleased your answer is yes. I wonder if you can start work on Friday at 4 p.m.? OK. I will wait to hear back from you tomorrow. Congratulations on your decision. I think you made a good one. I will have lots of information to give you about your orientation program when you call me tomorrow.*

Occasionally you may hear a reluctance to make an immediate commitment to the job. This could happen for several reasons. The person may have second thoughts about changing jobs or working for your store. Sometimes a job offer is used as leverage with the current employer to get a salary increase or some other concessions. If the candidate needs time to think about it, probe for reasons, offer additional information or assistance, and get a date and time when you will hear the person's decision. If by some chance, the person says "No," be sure to explore the reasons for this decision. These reasons could provide very helpful information in planning future interviews.

Put It in Writing

The document can be as simple as a form letter with the blanks filled in, or a check-list of information for the new staff person, or a standard letter. The style and formality seems to vary although the content includes:

- ○ job description or duties
- ○ salary
- ○ expected hours
- ○ start date
- ○ welcome and congratulations.

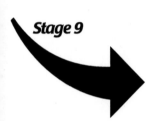

Notify and Thank Other Candidates

Next, contact the other candidates (if there are any) and let them know your decision.

I am calling to let you know that I have made my decision on the sales person for the store. Regrettably, you were not selected at this time. It was a very difficult decision because I had several very good candidates to choose from. Quite honestly, I feel the selected candidate fits a little bit better with our needs right now. I want to keep your résumé on file in case I add another person to the team in the near future. How would you feel about that? I appreciate that you will not sit around and wait. I would not expect you to do that. When I find talented people, I make a practice of following their career path. I wish you luck in finding the job opportunity you are looking for. Thank you once again for interviewing with us and for your interest in our store. Drop in and see us if you are in the neighbourhood.

Support the Transition to Your Store

All retailers meet with the new person as quickly as possible after the job offer is made to outline the details of employment, the transition period, plans for orientation, etc.

Managing the actual transition is important because it represents an opportunity to create a positive "first impression" for the employee as they begin to work and plan with you. Here are some things to keep in mind:

Be clear about the start date. Not all candidates will be able to begin immediately. Some may have obligations to their current employer. Do your best to minimize the delay, but be sensitive to the person's needs in this area.

Get started as soon as possible on the required paper work. If you are not familiar with the requirements for documentation (Revenue Canada, OHIP, etc.,) contact your retail association for advice.

Stay in touch! The person may be influenced to take another position or stay in their old job. If you are not available to provide information and help with the transition, you could lose this valuable new employee. Even if there is no pressure to consider other options, the employee will appreciate your attention and support in this period of transition.

CONGRATULATIONS

You have a new staff person. Although nine steps were required to select the right person from the applicants you started with, you can feel confident that your investment has resulted in hiring the best.

Orientation – Bringing the New Staff Up To Speed

8

This chapter will:

✓ emphasize the importance of the first weeks on the job

✓ describe five types of information that all new staff need

✓ give examples of a variety of approaches to make orientation more interesting and involving

✓ outline seven steps for developing a plan to help your new staff members learn what they need to know to be successful

WHAT DO YOU DO TO HELP NEW STAFF?

Use the following scale to assess your orientation practices:

0 points = never
1 point = occasionally
2 points = sometimes
3 points = frequently

____ 1. I use a checklist of what a new staff member needs to learn.

____ 2. I plan the timing and order of the orientation topics carefully to make it easier for the new staff to "learn the ropes."

____ 3. I provide important information about customer service, our business ethics and how our store does business.

____ 4. I make sure the new staff member has an opportunity to meet and spend time with other members of the staff.

____ 5. I include the basic information required for both selling and non-selling duties.

____ 6. I give the new staff member the opportunity to team up for a while with someone who has more experience.

____ 7. I limit new staff's contact with customers until they have an understanding of our business.

____ 8. I use a variety of different methods to help new staff learn about what is expected on the job.

____ 9. I am clear with the new staff member about exactly what is expected in the important selling and non-selling areas of the job.

____ 10. On Day 1, I am prepared and make a good impression.

____ **TOTAL SCORE**

Interpretation:

0 – 10   Your poor staff are on their own.

11 – 20   Some good things are happening. Do more.

21 – 30   You've got a real "learning organization." Keep it up!

ORIENTING NEW STAFF

Congratulations! You have a new staff person! The hard work of attracting promising applicants and selecting the right one is over! Now the fun really begins. How do you get this person off to a good start? How do you build on the enthusiasm and willingness to learn and the desire to make a good impression? How do you make sure that he or she spends time doing the things you think are important?

You want new staff to do a good job. The new staff wants that too. Even if they have worked in a store before, their lack of familiarity with your store, your customers and your methods makes this difficult. It's important that you bring them up to speed quickly! The way you do this, through work assignment, coaching and training is called "orientation."

Orientation usually begins **before the new person actually starts work.** The manager will tell the staff about the new person joining the team and begin to plan for the first day on the job.

First Impressions Are Lasting Ones

That first hour of the new job will leave a lasting impression or tone with the new person. Who provided the welcome? Was it warm and friendly? To whom was the newcomer introduced? Was the person left alone or did someone show the person around? Did learning start right away? Were people available and willing to answer questions? And on and on. It is very important to make the first impression that first day a meaningful and memorable one.

A Partnership

Orientation is a partnership that includes you, as the store manager, your new sales person, and your existing staff. Everyone wants this new person to be a great addition to the team. Who should do what and when? Everyone has something to offer. This is the time to work with the new staff because they are:

- ◯ open to new ideas

- ◯ expecting to learn

- ◯ aware of their own lack of knowledge

- ◯ insecure with their own lack of experience in your store

- ◯ eager to make a good impression.

Manager + New Staff Person + Store Staff

If you don't begin the orientation immediately, you will lose this wonderful opportunity to give helpful information and guidelines **while your sales person is eager to hear it.**

The high performing stores we interviewed know the importance of these moments of readiness in the new hire. These stores provide information and skill training even before the new person ever goes on to the selling floor. They use a couple of evenings and days to help new staff learn "how to do things around here." And they continue to orient staff for several weeks after they have been on the selling floor.

The range in estimates of the time required before staff are fully oriented was from 6 to 12 shifts for part-timers and one to two weeks for full-time staff. Retailers who have a large number of products report that it takes several months.

There are five important reasons for getting the person off to a good start:

○ to help the new person feel clear and comfortable about his or her duties as soon as possible

○ to make sure the new person begins to develop some confidence about what is expected

○ to help the team adapt to the new member

○ to make sure customer service is maintained

○ to be sure that store assets are secure.

Why

The new person is not the only one faced with having to adjust. Staff need to learn how this new person thinks and how he or she will fit in. And you, as manager, need to adjust your schedule to bring this person on board.

Every store is different. Every selling season is different. Every staff person is different. Orientation in each store will be different.

You have launched a new staff person off to a good start if **after the first week,** he or she:

○ knows what is important to you in the areas of customer service, business ethics, etc.

○ is clear about his or her duties and the standards expected

○ feels confident that the job can be learned and he or she can be successful

○ wants to continue to work in your store.

WHAT SHOULD BE INCLUDED IN THE ORIENTATION PROGRAM?

There are five types of information:

1. Immediate Personal Information

2. The Big Picture

3. The Practical Details

4. How We Sell and Service Customers

5. Product Knowledge

1. Immediate Personal Information

Start by considering your new staff person's most immediate needs. By starting here, you demonstrate that you expect them to consider others' needs – the customer's and yours.

When you first started in a new job, what did you want to know?

Ask your most recent staff what they would want to know if they were starting off again in the store. Likely they will tell you that new staff need personal information about:

- ❍ pay, benefits, bonuses, incentives, deductions, pay dates and methods

- ❍ selling duties and expectations

- ❍ expectations
    - ❍ dress code, personal grooming
    - ❍ what if they are late or sick
    - ❍ personal phone calls
    - ❍ non-selling duties

- ❍ working conditions
    - ❍ store hours, schedules, breaks
    - ❍ parking, public transportation
    - ❍ staff lockers, where to hang coats, etc.
    - ❍ vacation.

2. The "Big Picture"

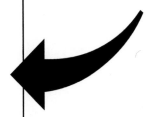

You will never be able to tell new staff everything they need to know for every situation that will come up. That's why many stores start with the "big picture." The "big picture" includes taking time to discuss your hopes and dreams for your store; the way your store fits into the bigger competitive picture; and the values, beliefs and principles that have made your store what it is today. The big picture includes objectives for sales, comparative profits (against last year) and market share.

It is information about these areas that will help your new staff members make decisions when they have to. If a member of your staff knows the reasons behind the policies, procedures, rules and day-to-day practices, he or she can usually figure out what should be done in a new situation. Therefore, be sure to take time to discuss:

○ why and when the store was started

○ what customers you serve

○ trends in store sales and revenue

○ why your store is unique
  ○ your competitive edge
  ○ your staff and great stories about their commitment to customers and sales
  ○ any policies (e.g. guarantees, returns, etc.) that make the store special
  ○ your values and beliefs about your products; the kind of relationship you want with customers, staff, and suppliers; your approach to sales, merchandising, etc.

Having a written statement about these items and what your store is all about, will make it even easier to share this with the new staff member.

3. The Practical Details

It is important to balance the "big picture" with the essentials and daily tasks. There are hundreds of practical details that are necessary in your store. If you haven't done so already, you should make a list of them. They could include areas such as:

○ Introductions: all staff, customers, mall security, delivery staff

○ Sales administration: how to ring up a sale, do a refund, exchange or credit, fill out packing/delivery slips

○ Inventory: how reordering is managed, receipt and processing of shipments, procedures for debit/credit cards, and stocking shelves

○ Merchandising: what signs we use and why, how we set up displays and why, what window treatments we prefer and why

○ Security: staff entrances, locking up, opening up, how to handle shoplifting

○ Safety: first aid materials and procedures, reporting accidents, fire alarm, emergency numbers

○ Housekeeping: where supplies are kept, expectations.

4. How We Sell and Service Customers

Many of the retailers interviewed teach their staff specific steps for selling and providing service in their stores. For example:

- ❍ How to acknowledge the customer
- ❍ How to approach the customer to find out what they want and need
- ❍ How to present the features and benefits to match the customer's needs
- ❍ How to close the sale.

You likely have your own model of the steps in selling. There are additional books on the subject in the bibliography at the back of this book.

When you link the practical details of daily work to your philosophy of customer service and to the standards in your store, you help new staff see how everything is connected.

Here are several examples of orientation messages other retailers give.

- ❍ *Our customers don't like to wait in line. Therefore, try to ring up sales within two minutes from the time the customer comes to the cash, or apologize for the delay.*

- ❍ *Our customers appreciate suggestions, so when we ring up a sale, we note their likes and dislikes quickly in the computer in this section ... or we make a note later. Read your customer notes whenever you can. If you see someone come in that you served last week, check your notes if you can, before you approach them.*

- ❍ *Our customers like service and we benefit by helping them find the right goods. So you need to know our stock, where it is, and how to show it off. In this store, you bring the right size to the customer on the floor or in fitting rooms. You help them look at options and at co-ordinates.*

---

5. Product Knowledge

How do you tell the difference between true sales people and order-takers? According to John Lawhon in *Selling Retail,* true sales people know their products and are able to help customers learn about the products that will meet their needs. Order-takers don't sell.

Learning product information never ends as you can see from the list of what is included in this category.

Product Information

- ○ What are the features and benefits

- ○ What do the products cost (how much excitement can staff generate if they have to keep looking at price tags?)

- ○ Where was the product made, by what company, from what materials

- ○ How is the product used

- ○ What choices are available (sizes, shapes, colours, textures etc)

- ○ What other products compete with this product and how do the features and benefits compare

- ○ What are the best sellers in the store

- ○ What are the specialty items

- ○ Which items are returned most frequently and why

- ○ What is being advertised by your store and by the competition

- ○ What is in stock and what is coming in

- ○ What can be ordered and when would orders come in

- ○ Where to get product information

The Canadian Booksellers Association has done some interesting research. The survey results showed that of the employees in bookstores that responded to the questionnaire, over 85 percent considered the following as part of product knowledge:

- ○ knowing stock

- ○ knowing titles

- ○ knowing how to access information

- ○ knowing what product is coming into the store that may be of interest to the customer

- ○ general knowledge

How Does A New Staff Person Begin the Never-Ending Product-Learning

In helping new staff learn about products, you are helping them learn two things: the product information and how to find and learn it on a continuing basis. The most effective ways are to assign a variety of tasks.

○ Ask the new hire to read all the printed material on a selection of the store products (e.g. manufacturer's information, brochures, consumer reports, trade magazines, popular magazines, journals).

○ Suggest the new hire talk to people (e.g. other staff, manufacturer's representatives, sales managers at suppliers, service people who repair products you sell, customers) in order to find the answers to a list of questions you think are important.

○ Ask the new hire to examine the product closely and describe it in detail to you at a later date (e.g. How is it made? Why is it made that way? What materials make it strong, attractive, easy to use).

○ Ask staff to team with the new hire to deepen interest and expertise (e.g. colour psychology, types of wood, types of book binding, sport shoe design).

HOW TO PASS THE INFORMATION ALONG AND MAKE IT INTERESTING

There are many ways that a new staff member can learn about your store. Don't assume that it must all be done by you in a face-to-face environment. In fact a new person might find this approach pretty overwhelming. Instead, try to break up the orientation by using . . .

○ a variety of approaches (see below)

○ different sources of information (people, books, activities, etc.)

○ different times (scheduled over the first days on the job)

Before we present a variety of approaches for helping the new hire learn, it is important to explain an over-all approach to learning. No matter what someone is learning, CPR is what ensures the learning lasts. What is CPR?

C Check-up. Follow-up to ensure the information was understood, the agreements made were followed through.

P Provide opportunities for practice and for feedback. Learning a skill requires both. Changing a habit requires time for trying out or practising new ways and feedback on trial practices.

R Reinforcement and recognition. People need to know that their efforts to learn are seen and valued as well as their success in mastering new ways of doing things.

As you read the variety of approaches and think about how to schedule them into the first weeks of orientation, build CPR into your schedule and theirs.

Variety of Approaches and Sources

Some of the approaches you might want to try include:

○ Direct instruction from you (the obvious).

○ Encourage the new staff member to spend time watching you and other members of the staff doing specific tasks.

○ Partner the newcomer with other member(s) of the staff and have them work closely together on specific skills (eg. paperwork, taking measurements).

○ Get the new staff member to work with customers on specific tasks.

○ Assign reading of written information about products, policies, and procedures.

○ Test the new staff member on product information; quizzes can be developed by other staff.

○ Demonstrate selling techniques.

○ Role-play difficult scenarios (e.g. angry customers).

○ Ask the newcomer to memorize product locations and prices.

○ Ask the new staff member to check out certain things on their own (e.g. explore the stock room, walk through the rest of the commercial area, check out the competition, etc.)

With the variety of things a new hire needs to learn, and the different approaches to making the information available, no wonder you need a plan.

Here are Some Creative Approaches from Retailers

Examples

○ New staff receive the checklist that their managers are using to guide their orientation. Both check off what has been done on the list after it has been completed. Both are responsible for orientation.

○ The telephone is the last thing that new staff are exposed to. Unless they are very familiar with the store and the stock, it will be frustrating for them and they will provide poor service to the customer.

○ Out loud, in front of other staff, invite the newcomer to ask them about their first days on the job, about the best sellers, about customers and about what it's like to work with you!

○ Lunch breaks are used to get acquainted and continue the learning.

○ One store developed an orientation activity that resembled a scavenger hunt. The new hire was given a list of questions that could be answered by talking to other staff members or simply by observing the store in operation. They had to write their answers to the questions and explain where they found the answers. It was a lot more interesting and allowed the new person to take initiative to find answers.

○ One retailer has written out ten descriptions of customer requests and has new staff read each one, search for the merchandise, and come and tell the manager what four or five items would be worth showing to the customer. Further, the staff person is asked to describe the features and benefits of each item.

○ Another asks new staff to compare his product with that of a competitor and gives them categories so they can learn to compare features, benefits, product composition, price, guarantee, service. New staff are encouraged to ask current staff for help.

○ One retailer has a small collection of training videos and motivational audio tapes.

○ Tell stories about excellent customer service. The stories reinforce your values and instil pride.

○ Another retailer keeps a file of testimonials from customers for the new hire to read.

○ Another retailer provide two lists: A GREEN list identifies "Must Do." A RED list identifies "No-No." These are reviewed during orientation and referred to as standards for performance – expected behaviour – thereafter.

○ Staff are introduced to people so they feel welcomed.

Timing

You can't tell the new person everything at once. It is important to plan what you will introduce the first day, the next two days, within a week, and by the end of the month. The end of this chapter outlines a method to plan orientation. Take the time to do a plan, and share it with the new and old staff. They are your partners in making it happen.

DAY 1 HOUR 1

Begin by establishing the rapport. "Bill, I'd like to tell you that you don't need to make believe you know all about your job today. We know you know less about your job today than any day you'll be on the job. So we welcome you, and I want to tell you the most important information you'll need to be successful here. You're already a member of our team. You don't have to get to know us before you can feel free to count on us. We assume the best of you. We're glad you're on our team; that's important. You can't prove yourself in one day; it will take time, so just relax. We're with you. We're on your side, and we recognize you're on our side."

Managing by Influence
Kenneth and Linda Schatz
Prentice Hall 1986

A SAMPLE ORIENTATION CHECKLIST

Use the sample checklists as starting points in designing your own checklist for new staff members.

What A Staff Person Needs to Know	How can a new staff person learn about this?	When does the new staff person need to learn this?
○ **About our customers:** ○ Target market ○ Customer profile ○ Desired customers ○ Features that make them choose us		
○ **How do we handle:** ○ ringing up a sale ○ damaged product on the shelf ○ receipt of shipments ○ shipping shorts & longs ○ tagging ○ shoplifting ○ returns		
○ **About our products:** ○ what do we sell ○ what are best sellers ○ where is everything located ○ where is stock kept & how is it organized ○ what are each item's features/benefits ○ what things go well together		
○ **About our information systems:** ○ what is on the price tag ○ what gets recorded in a sale ○ what gets recorded in a refund ○ how do we track product volume ○ how do we track customer preferences ○ how do we note shorts before we are out		
○ **Housekeeping:** ○ where to find equipment ○ when to vacuum, dust ○ procedures for garbage		
○ **About our team** ○ how to cover for each other ○ what to do if unable to take a shift ○ who to go to for advice/assistance		

A SAMPLE ORIENTATION CHECKLIST

What A Staff Person Needs to Know About Customer Service How To:	How can a new staff person learn about this?	When does the new staff person need to learn this?
How To: ○ make the customer feel important ○ listen and respond to customer's feelings ○ ask effective questions to determine customer's needs ○ offer suggestions		
○ acknowledge the customer ○ give customer full attention ○ make sure the customer is satisfied ○ use telephone etiquette		
○ deal with unrealistic customer expectations ○ problem solve (i.e. deal with customer complaints) ○ deal with angry customers ○ use non-verbal communications – from eye contact to service-oriented posture		
○ have empathy ○ show willingness to serve ○ demonstrate caring and helpfulness		
○ know merchandise and services ○ follow-through ○ know store policies, procedures		

DEVELOPING YOUR OWN ORIENTATION CHECKLIST

Every store is different. Tailor your orientation to your store and your resources.

There are seven steps to an orientation plan that will serve you through several new hires. If you complete the first four steps, you will be ready for any new hire that comes in.

Step 1:

On pieces of paper, write down everything someone has to know to be successful in your store. At this stage, don't worry about when or how the items you list will be learned: in the next step you will sort each item into a schedule. Just write one item per piece of paper. Use scrap or small post it notes. Imagine what happens in the store from the moment it opens until it closes and list everything that a staff person needs to know. Think about selling and non-selling tasks. You could have anywhere between 50 and 100 pieces of paper. It will take about 15 minutes to complete most of this step. You could also ask your staff to jot down items on different pieces of paper.

How to handle ringing up a sale	How to handle complaints	Where are different products located?
Who changes displays and when	Reporting in sick	What are the best sellers?
Chewing Gum	Shoplifting	Where to find stock

Step 2:

Begin to think about when different things need to be learned. Find some empty space on a desk or counter or the floor. Designate several areas for sorting the pieces of paper from Step 1 into three piles. Sort the pieces of paper according to when (Week One, Week Two, Week Three) you think would be a good time to introduce staff to the item.

After sorting into weeks, take all the slips of paper in the area you have designated as "Week One" and sort them into piles for each day. Start with Day One and ask yourself: What can the staff person learn and do successfully (and without risk to the store)? Go on to Day Two, Three, Four, etc.

Step 3:

Look at the items in Week One and put a symbol on the ones that you will need to review once or twice after the new hire has been introduced to them. Notice we said "has been introduced to them" because we do not think you are going to do it all! There are other staff. There is product literature, self-teaching questions, and a variety of other methods described on the next two pages. More about that later.

Step 4:

Make your plan by calendar date. Take the sheets for Day One and list them on one page called Day One and so on. In the early days of a job, the new hire is introduced to a lot of information. Be sure to schedule time for the person to review and ask questions about items that were introduced earlier in the week.

Step 5:

Implement your plan.

Step 6:

Review Week One and discuss it with the new hire. What went well? What took more time/less time than you thought? What is clear? What needs more time?

Step 7:

Revise your calendar based on your experience and on the feedback you got in Step 6.

Repeat Steps 6 and 7 after Week Two and Week Three.

WEEK ONE	DAY ONE	DAY TWO	DAY THREE	DAY FOUR	DAY FIVE	DAY SIX	DAY SEVEN
	☐	☐	☐ review…	☐	☐	☐ review…	☐
	☐	☐	☐	☐	☐	☐	☐
	☐	☐	☐	☐	☐	☐	☐
	☐	☐	☐	☐	☐	☐	☐
	☐	☐	☐	☐	☐	☐	☐
	☐	☐	☐	☐	☐	☐	☐

WEEK TWO	DAY ONE	DAY TWO	DAY THREE	DAY FOUR	DAY FIVE	DAY SIX	DAY SEVEN
	☐	☐	☐ review...	☐	☐	☐ review...	☐
	☐	☐	☐	☐	☐	☐	☐
	☐	☐	☐	☐	☐	☐	☐
	☐	☐	☐	☐	☐	☐	☐
	☐	☐	☐	☐	☐	☐	☐
	☐	☐	☐	☐	☐	☐	☐

DEVELOPING HIGH PERFORMING STAFF

Coaching and Training

9

This chapter will:

✓ help you identify the learning styles of your staff

✓ describe a three-step model for effective on-the-spot coaching, and a three-part model for follow-up

✓ provide specific examples of how to coach on real issues

✓ offer alternative ways to respond when staff are not receptive to coaching

✓ provide a method for planning staff meetings

✓ describe a format for meetings to review past store results and plan for up-coming weeks

✓ provide a list of exciting, useful training ideas used by retailers

HELPING STAFF LEARN

Read each item on the left below and check off one box that best reflects your assessment.

How well do you think you do the following?	I am doing this well	I am doing this ok	I need to give this more attention	This is not relevant to me
1. I ask my staff what they need to learn.				
2. I assess what my staff need to learn by noticing how they do their work.				
3. I act as a coach every day, helping my staff learn and grow.				
4. I encourage staff to coach each other.				
5. I ask staff to observe me doing some task and give me feedback on it.				
6. I set a good example by taking time to learn and develop my skills.				
7. I invite staff to play the part of a customer so I can demonstrate ways to sell and provide customer service.				
8. I play the part of a customer or supplier and ask staff to practise their skills with me.				
9. I ask questions that help staff think about their own methods for doing things.				
10. I look for ways to give my staff detailed feedback and encouragement on a daily basis.				
11. I follow up after a coaching or training session to support learning and provide reinforcement.				
12. I plan meetings that will be fun and help staff learn.				
13. I conduct fun and informative meetings.				
TOTAL CHECK MARKS				
Multiply by	multiply by 3	multiply by 2	multiply by 1	multiply by 0
TOTAL SCORE				
GRAND TOTAL – add total scores of columns 1 + 2 + 3				

Interpretation:

0 – 13   You are not investing very much in your essential resources.

14 – 26   This chapter will support your intentions to help staff learn.

27 – 39   This chapter will reinforce what you are doing and give you some additional ideas.

CONTINUOUS LEARNING IS THE NAME OF THE GAME

New staff are not the only ones who need to do a lot of learning. New products, new services, new technologies, new suppliers and new competitors, and hopefully, new customers mean that learning is the name of the game. Along with the constant pressure of other sales activities, you and your staff have a lot of learning to do.

Every successful retailer has to be a top-notch coach and skilled trainer. Not only that, you need to teach your staff to coach each other. Why? Because your success and your profits depend on the abilities of your staff. You need staff to be at their best every minute of every selling day. This is a challenge. The reality is that human beings have "ups and downs" or "highs and lows" every day. Does this mean that you are at the whim of the moods of your staff? If your answer is "YES," then you probably don't see yourself in much of a coaching role – yet! If your answer is "NO," then you already know that you can influence what goes on every day in your store through coaching.

What Is Coaching? What Is Training?

Let's be clear on the definition of terms. COACHING is usually done one-on-one, in an informal, spontaneous way. It is focused on how to improve performance and provides recognition of good performance. Think of it as on-the-spot demonstrations, role-plays and trial practices. In contrast, TRAINING is usually scheduled, and often done in a group in an informal or formal manner. There is usually preparation ahead of the session.

Both are about helping people learn.

It Is a Coaching Moment! It Is a Training Event!

HOW DO STAFF LEARN?

Imagine that you had to assemble a bicycle. What would you do first? Read the instructions? Look at the diagram? Take all the pieces out of the box and sort them? Talk to someone else about how to proceed? We each have preferences regarding how we learn. Generally we are more comfortable and effective learning in one or two of the following:

○ Some learn by **seeing** things
(seeing the product, watching a demonstration of how to handle an objection, observing a sale, reading a product brochure, viewing a movie or video, etc.)

○ Some learn by **hearing** things
(listening to you talk about the product, hearing an interchange with a customer, hearing an audio tape, hearing a presentation on security, etc.)

○ Some learn by **doing** things
(touching and handling merchandise to see how it works, writing up a sales order or refund slip, unpacking boxes and loading shelves, rearranging items on displays, etc.)

Knowing about these different styles will make it easier for you to coach and train your staff. If you give a "visual" person a **talk** on how to fill out a sales slip, you will not have their attention. If you make a "doer" sit still while you **show them a demonstration** you will drive them crazy. Don't ask someone who learns best by hearing to **read** the new product pamphlets. Instead, team the person up with someone and ask them to prepare to teach others – they will have to talk and listen to the information in order to be able to teach it.

Which is your preferred style of learning? Be careful not to impose your preferred learning style on your staff. Think about each staff person and ask yourself how each one prefers to learn. You may be surprised that you already know. You can also find out by asking them:

Which way do you prefer to learn new product information? Would you prefer to: (1) read about it; (2) watch a video on it; (3) listen to someone tell you about it; (4) ask someone questions about it; or (5) handle it and figure out how it works? I'm asking so that I can get a better understanding of your preferences. Do you want me to repeat the alternatives? Are there others you would add?

What would be the best way for you to learn more about teamwork? Would you prefer to read about it, watch a video, listen to a lecture, ask questions, ask other people about it, do a role-play or discuss a situation that could arise in a team?

SKILLS FOR COACHING AND TRAINING

Most of the skills required to be successful at coaching and training are the same:

○ Communication skills, which include listening, asking questions, providing instructions, giving and receiving feedback, and acknowledging feelings.

○ Problem solving skills, which include assessing, collecting information, suggesting solutions, considering options, trying or testing, making decisions, and implementing them.

You also have to be knowledgeable about the area you are helping someone to learn.

At this moment, you have all of these skills in varying degrees. Refer back to your self-assessments in Chapters 2, 3, 4, and 5. You solve problems every single day, and you know more about retail than anyone else in your store. So that means you are able to be a coach and a trainer. Do you want to be? Are you ready?

Styles of management are described in Chapter 10.

A COACHING MODEL THAT WORKS – ACT

The acronym ACT is intended to get you moving – to take action **now!** It stands for:

A - ASSESS (listen, observe, analyze, evaluate performance)

- ❍ What is the staff person doing?
- ❍ What impact is he or she having?
- ❍ What's working?
- ❍ What could be improved?
- ❍ What style of management does this person need?
- ❍ How does this person learn best?
- ❍ What will be helpful now?

C - COMMUNICATE (ask questions, provide feedback, clarify meaning, acknowledge feelings)

- ❍ Ask what happened.
- ❍ Ask what was intended.
- ❍ Tell what you saw and heard.
- ❍ Discuss the impact of the situation on the customer, on you, and on staff.
- ❍ Inquire about the beliefs behind the actions.
- ❍ Invite thinking about alternatives.
- ❍ Give feedback, support, and praise.

T - TEACH OPTIONS (for the situation)

- ❍ Ask questions that lead to learning.
- ❍ Explore options, alternatives for the situation.
- ❍ Demonstrate how to do something.
- ❍ Provide resources.
- ❍ Role-play.
- ❍ Experiment.

The manager of the future will simply be a learning guide.

Peter Drucker

ACT + CPR =
HIGH
PERFORMANCE

Then follow up later by providing opportunities for practice and feedback on new behaviour. Apply the CPR model:

- ○ **C**heck-up to ensure there is understanding and to support the learning. Ensure there is follow-through on commitments

- ○ **P**rovide feedback and, where appropriate, practice

- ○ **R**ecognize the effort and the results.

Introduction to Coaching Examples

As you read the following examples, several questions will likely come to mind.

What is the most appropriate location for a coaching conversation? Should it take place in the store, where other staff and customers might notice, or in the back room?

Of course, your response would depend on the content of the coaching moment. It would also depend on your beliefs about learning and about mistakes. If you believe that mistakes are incidents to hide, or that making a mistake is shameful, then the discussion should take place in the back room.

If you believe that:

- ○ learning is something everyone does and should do

- ○ mistakes are opportunities for learning

- ○ we need each other to be mirrors so we can see ourselves

- ○ the only way to learn interpersonal skills (teamwork, customer service, sales, negotiation, etc.) is to get feedback and try different approaches

- ○ customers and staff respect the attention people give to developing skills,

then coaching would happen in the open. Only highly personal reprimands would happen in the back room.

Take coaching
conversations
out of the closet.

138

A second question you might have as you read the examples is about timing. When should a manager intervene in a conversation between a salesperson and a customer? If the manager sees that a sale is not going well, should he or she step in? When should the manager wait to see if the salesperson can turn the conversation around without the manager's help? You will have to weigh the value of the customer and the sale, the potential for recovery after the conversation, the likelihood that the salesperson will be able to change the conversation before it ends, the impact of intervening, and the learning that could happen from your actions.

INTRODUCTION TO COACHING EXAMPLES

Each example provides part of a conversation. Assume that the desired outcomes are to:

○ encourage the staff person to change his or her behaviour (skills, knowledge, actions, etc.)

○ support the staff person's motivation to learn

○ develop the staff person's learning and problem solving skills

○ keep the communication lines open.

> *Effective communication = content outcomes + relationship outcomes*

It's a Coaching Moment

It's Monday morning and Larry is late again. It's time to ACT.

Manager: *Larry, good morning. Can I talk to you for a minute? I see that you're late again today. That is the fourth time. Do you remember we talked about this last week and the week before?*

Larry: *Yes, yes, I know and I'm really sorry. I don't intend to be late. I just have a hard time waking up. The alarm goes off, I put it on snooze for five minutes, I fall back asleep and then I'm late. Don't worry, it won't happen again.*

> *What would you say now?*

Manager: *I appreciate you don't intend to be late. How can you be sure that it won't happen again?*

Larry: *I don't know. I'll figure out a way.*

Manager: *I would be willing to help you find a way so that we won't be having this discussion again. Would you be willing to try a few things?*

Larry: *Sure.*

Manager: *How about getting an alarm clock with a louder alarm? How about moving the clock out of your reach, so that you have to get out of bed to turn it off? How about getting a friend to call you to be sure you are up and moving? Would any of those suggestions work for you?*

Larry:	The one about moving the clock away from the bed appeals to me. I'll try that.
Manager:	OK. I'm glad that you're willing to try something different to solve this problem. I hope it works. I'd like you to consider one more thing. Are you willing?
Larry:	Sure, I guess so. What did you have in mind?
Manager:	When you're late, the other staff have to pitch in and cover for you. That really puts an unfair burden on them - it's happened four times now. What can you do to demonstrate that you understand you have inconvenienced them?
Larry:	I'll apologize.
Manager:	I'm not sure they'll accept that as meaningful after four times. (PAUSE)
Larry:	I'll offer to do all the vacuuming this week.

What would you say now?

The manager would check during the week, provide feedback and recognize Larry's efforts. If there had been no change, the manager would ACT again.

More Coaching Moments

It's Tuesday afternoon and you just saw Mary responding poorly to an angry customer. The customer left abruptly. It's time to ACT.

Manager:	Mary, I overheard the conversation you had with that customer. You sure sounded frustrated.
Mary:	I get so mad when people treat me that way. Who does she think I am anyway?
Manager:	I appreciate your feelings. She did sound like she got out of bed on the wrong side this morning. (PAUSE) I wonder what else it could mean?
Mary:	Maybe she had a fight with her husband or maybe she couldn't find a parking space in the mall. Who knows?
Manager:	Or maybe she was disappointed that the sweater didn't hold its shape after she washed it. Did you hear her say that?
Mary:	Yeah, I heard her, but she sure didn't have to treat me as if it were my fault.
Manager:	(Acknowledge feelings) I don't like it when someone speaks to me in a really angry way, especially when I haven't been the cause of the situation. I appreciate what you are saying. (PAUSE) Let's look at what you might do differently in the future that might help you and the customer. I wonder what would have happened if you had said something like: "I can tell you are really upset. You sound

disappointed that the sweater didn't wash well. What can we do to satisfy this situation? You could say: "I am very sorry that you got this sweater. Let's find you a replacement." You could say: "Our policy is satisfaction guaranteed. Would you like a refund or exchange?" Which one of those might work for you?

Mary: *I don't know right now. Probably they are all possibilities. One thing I know for sure. I need to learn how to handle these kinds of situations better.*

Manager: *Yes, I agree with you. It is hard on you and impacts on your ability to serve customers. When I'm faced with this type of situation, I ask myself a question: Is this customer mad at me or the situation? What else could this mean? It helps me focus on things other than my hurt feelings. Would you be willing to try it?*

Mary: *Sure I would. Thanks.*

Manager: *I'm confident that you'll get more skilful. Let's talk about it and maybe we can role-play some situations in a few days. In the meantime, I see you are still a bit upset. What would help you shift gears? Fixing the front display table? Putting some stock back?*

Assess
Communicate
Teach

More Coaching Moments

It's Wednesday evening and you just saw Nick lose a sale because he didn't deal with the customer's objection. It's time to ACT.

Manager: *Say Nick, I saw that sale get away from you. What happened?*

Nick: *Oh, you saw it. I don't know. Everything seemed to be going OK and then he turned and walked out. It all happened so quickly.*

Manager: *What part do you remember?*

Nick: *Well, I remember him asking about the colour choices and the sizes...and then...oh yeah...he said he didn't like the colours. And then before I could say anything, he was gone.*

Manager: *Did you notice anything earlier in your discussion that would be a clue? As you know, people are always giving us nonverbal signals or clues as well as verbal ones. Did you notice any clues?*

Nick: *Yeah, now that you mention it, I do remember him rejecting the red and yellow without even considering them.*

Manager: *Good observation. That would have been a good spot to say: "The red and yellow don't appeal to you. What is your colour preference? Or, what are you trying to match this with? Or, tell me some more about your room. Or, have you considered a plaid with a variety of colours?"*

Nick: *Umm. Yes, that does make sense. I lost the sale because I didn't respond to his clues. I didn't find a way to ask him questions that would keep him engaged in conversation long enough so that I could suggest alternatives - not to mention some add-ons.*

Manager: *I find that when the customer is asking me questions, it doesn't give me an opportunity to learn much about his needs. So I try to turn the conversation around so I can ask him questions. Does that make sense? Let's pretend right now that I am the customer. Try an approach to see if it works for you.*

CPR
Check-up
Provide practice and feedback
Recognize the effort and the results.

FOLLOW UP

Remember, for new ideas and skills to be integrated, people need CPR. Your CPR breathes recall into forgetfulness. It stimulates action when there is apathy. It develops motivation in the disheartened.

How to Begin a Coaching Moment When There is Resistance

Not every staff person will be as open-minded as Larry, Mary and Nick. How do you begin a coaching moment if you have a person who's not receptive? What can you do when you get a response like:

> *"I'm busy right now, can we talk later?"* or *"I am going on break right now"?*

Assess your reaction to these staff comments. Do you regard them as inappropriate? Are you saying to yourself: "A manager should not stand for that kind of a response from staff"? You may be correct. A lot depends on the tone of the response and on past relationships between the staff person and the manager. A lot depends on whether you believe staff should jump when the manager makes a request, and if they do not, that they are being impudent.

You have two options.

Do you want to deal with the issue you originally wanted to talk about? Or, do you want to set that aside, and deal with your feelings about the staff person's response to your request? To which one do you want to draw attention? Which one will impact the most on business and motivation?

Here are some manager responses to consider:

○ *I can appreciate that you are busy. When would be a convenient time to talk* **today?** *I have some suggestions I would like you to consider.*

○ *You are right. It is break time. I will be available when you come back. This is important to me.*

○ *I'd like to join you on your break so that we can talk about it while it's fresh in both our minds.*

○ *I noticed you seem to be struggling with* _____. *I used to struggle with that one myself. I have some ideas. When would you like to hear them?*

○ *I appreciate that you don't want my help right now. Perhaps talking to Steve would help. He deals with that situation every day and has found a new way of approaching it.*

○ **When you** *lose a sale,* **I feel** *disappointed* **because** *you lost, the customer lost and the store lost. This is worth discussing now.*

○ *I can understand you are too upset to talk about it now. How long are you going to stay upset and have it impact on other customers and staff? Can you afford to be upset much longer?*

Which responses model the way the manager wants staff to behave when a customer responds in an unreceptive way?

How Does Coaching Affect You?

What are the implications of an ACT and CPR approach to developing your staff? The major implications are:

1. To see what is happening, you need to be there.

2. To talk about what happened and what could happen next time, you need to be there.

3. To check or follow up, provide feedback and recognition, you need to be there.

"Being there" means both physically and mentally. When you are in the store, you see what is happening. In juggling all your priorities, coaching is often the ball you drop. Nothing replaces your personal coaching, but you can only do so much of it.

4. You need to develop ACT and CPR skills among your staff so that they can and will coach each other.

As you think about developing staff skills in coaching, it's time to talk about training as another form of helping staff learn.

JUST BECAUSE YOU GOT TO THE TOP, DON'T THINK YOU CAN LET OFF STEAM ANY TIME YOU WANT. REMEMBER THAT WHEN YOU DO, THAT'S WHEN YOU ARE THE MOST LIKELY TO BE HARPOONED!

Be there

TRAINING THROUGH STAFF MEETINGS

Now let's shift gears from coaching moments to training events, and from individuals to groups.

There are a variety of settings for learning in a group. There are sessions called training workshops. There are conferences and there are staff meetings.

In all the interviews we conducted with successful retailers, they described the staff meeting as the most effective way to train their staff. Staff meetings happen more frequently than conferences or training sessions. The potential for learning is huge. It will be realized only if you plan your meetings more to help staff learn than to "get through an agenda." When you set up meetings, you consider the items you want to address. Do you also think about the best ways to address them?

- Whenever you think you should present information (e.g. product information or a procedure), consider asking staff to prepare and do it for you. Think of a staff member who is knowledgeable, or a staff member who would benefit from development in this area. In the first instance, you recognize expertise by asking the person to teach the rest of the staff. In the second instance, you provide a chance to learn. People learn a lot when they have to be responsible for teaching others. Assign it to one person or to a team who can work together.

- Whenever you want staff to give you ideas, challenge everyone to come up with as many as possible. Prime the pump, to get people's creative juices flowing:

  - Ask people to take a few moments to jot down their ideas before the people who usually speak offer theirs.

  - Ask people to pair up and have a competition to generate the most ideas about the topic (e.g. unusual uses for one of your products).

  - In addition to asking for realistic ideas, stretch their thinking by asking for at least one boring and one brilliant idea, or one "weary" and one "way out" idea.

- Whenever you want to develop staff skills, provide time for practice. Give people a sample situation to solve, and break into groups of two or three to role-play.

- Whenever you want to have a celebration, do it! Occasionally, ask staff to organize it.

Your brain thinks learning and problem solving are the same. Shouldn't we plan meetings to be as interesting as good training sessions?

A staff meeting planner is provided to help you think about the agenda items, the type of learning you want to take place, the best methods to use, and who can provide leadership.

A blank form is provided on page 152.

STAFF MEETING PLANNER

Time required	Agenda item	What do you want staff to learn? What do you want to learn?	Method to use	Who to involve
10 min.	Markdowns – review of last time	Want staff to learn about each other's perceptions of what went well and how we can improve	Group discussion	Lee & Joanne to lead
10 min.	Markdowns - new procedure	Want staff to understand the purpose of a new procedure ○ how it will address the complaints they had about the old procedure ○ and the steps involved	Presentation followed by questions	Manager & Moe who helped refine the new procedure
10 min.	Markdowns – practise new procedure	Want staff to get comfortable with the new procedure and know what to do in unusual situations	Examples of situations (i.e. case studies)	Manager and Moe
2 min	Schedule for implementing new procedure	Want everyone to know (learn) who has responsibility for what and when	Handout	Manager
20 min	Customer service	Want staff to appreciate that customer service applies to relations inside the store between different functions	Video	Joe to arrange

Videos are available from the Canadian Booksellers Association, the Canadian Retail Hardware Association, the Retail Learning Initiative and the Retail Council of Canada.

The next section also provides a plan for a meeting. It focuses on meetings that review past results, celebrate successes, identify areas for improvement and plan for the future.

A Format for Planning Staff Meetings

Agenda

1. Welcome & Purpose

2. Last Week's Results

3. Areas for Improvement

4. Information Sharing &/or Skill Development

5. Targets for Next Week

6. Summary & Recap of Assignments

7. Evaluation of the Meeting

When people go to meetings, they often wonder:

○ Will I be involved?

○ Will other people participate?

○ Will the same people do all the talking?

○ Will it be the same as all the other meetings we have?

○ Will it be fun?

○ Will we get the information we want to get?

○ Will it be worth my time?

Here is an agenda for a successful staff meeting.

1. Welcome and Purpose:

Set the tone for the meeting. Raise expectations for an interesting and productive session.

Talk about what you expect will happen by the end of the meeting.

I expect you'll all be as pleased as I am with the new merchandise I'm going to show you for next season.

We'll make a schedule of who is going to present the features and benefits of various items to us over the next few weeks.

By the end of our meeting, we all should be clear about the new procedure and be willing to monitor it over the next month.

Talk about the **items on the agenda.** As you list the agenda items tell staff which ones are for staff information only, which ones will be discussed, which need decisions, and which ones are for planning purposes.

2. Last Week's Results

○ What was great about last week? What did we do well ? When a week has been successful, staff will readily talk about their achievements. When a week has not been very rewarding, staff may need your help to keep energy levels up and to find the positive things that happened. Whatever went well deserves recognition. Even if things have gone poorly, there are always positive things to recognize. Help staff find them by asking questions.

○ What did our customers say about us?

○ What did we improve?

○ What did we learn?

○ Who gets compliments and rewards?

When you have used this format several times, staff will become comfortable with it and will be able to be lead parts of the meeting.

For variety, you could put a pile of different objects (e.g. pencil, key ring, stapler, garbage pail, coat, credit card, magazine, etc.) in the middle of a table and ask staff to take two minutes to choose an object which, based on its shape and colour and use, could represent what the week has been like.

These kinds of activities take about 10 minutes for a group of 7 to 10 people. They are not only fun, they stimulate thinking and creativity.

3. Areas for Improvement

Ask staff to identify what could be improved in the following areas:

○ communication

○ customer service

○ results

○ merchandising

Great athletic teams know: To play and win together, you must practise together

4. Information Sharing and/or Skill Development

This part of the meeting focuses on staff development. Topics include:

○ new product information

○ new ideas or plans

○ selling techniques

○ customer service strategies

○ a "how-to" demonstration

In the next section you will find dozens of ideas from retailers who use different ways to conduct this part of a staff meeting.

Goals are motivating

5. Create New Targets for the Coming Week

What are we most excited about and committed to:

○ for our customers this week?

○ for our store this week?

○ for the company this week?

○ for each other this week?

6. Summary and Recap of Assignments

Does everyone understand their responsibilities?

Does everyone understand our overall goal and plan?

7. Evaluation of the Meeting

Ask staff for feedback on the meeting.

○ Quick methods for response include thumbs up or down, hands up or down. Or, provide one piece of paper with open questions or categories to circle.

○ Rate this meeting using a scale of 1 = poor/low and 10 = excellent/high, in terms of quality of information, usefulness of discussion, its effectiveness, efficiency, and your enjoyment.

○ What was useful? Not so useful? Interesting?

○ What should we STOP doing, START doing, CONTINUE doing?

This format for a meeting is very effective. Everyone is involved and participates, which builds the team. The manager could conduct the whole meeting OR part of it OR rotate the responsibility among the staff OR ask people to volunteer for the part they want to conduct. The possibilities are endless.

The Timing and Duration of Staff Meetings

With seven-days-a-week shopping and the number of evenings your store is open, it's challenging to find an appropriate time to schedule staff meetings. Different retailers address this in different ways:

○ Some retailers hold no meetings at all. These people have lots of daily interaction and chatting back and forth.

○ Some hold mini-meetings for 10 to 15 minutes when the shift changes.

○ Some hold daily staff meetings for 30 minutes.

○ Some hold weekly training meetings for one hour.

○ Some hold monthly training meetings for two to three hours.

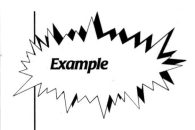
Example

A retailer with a large staff (30 to 50) provides 45 minutes of training **every morning and every evening** except Boxing Day. Half the staff (including managers) attend in the morning and the rest in the evening. The training is divided into thirds: one-third focuses on customer service and company values, one-third focuses on product knowledge and one-third is devoted to selling skills. Staff LOVE the quick sessions. Other retailers are constantly trying to hire their staff.

Are Staff Paid for Meetings?

An interesting question. Do you pay staff to attend staff meetings? Training sessions?

The retailers we interviewed said they pay for staff training and meetings because:

- ○ *Paying enables us to require staff attendance.*

- ○ *Staff regard it as work time and take it more seriously when they realize we are paying.*

- ○ *Paying is the fair thing to do.*

- ○ *Paying communicates a message to staff that learning is important to us.*

- ○ *Paying for meetings is an investment in the success of our business.*

TRAINING IDEAS FROM SUCCESSFUL RETAILERS

Bring in Guests

Examples

- ○ Invite a guest to your training event - a supplier to demonstrate a product.

- ○ Invite another store manager to speak about customer service or business values, market trends, new business, etc.

- ○ Bring in a community person whose specialty relates to your products (e.g. a teacher to a bookstore, a nurse to talk about safety, community police to talk about security).

- ○ Invite the owner to make a presentation at a training session.

Use Resources

- ○ Show a video about a product or customer service or selling skills, etc.

- ○ Create a lending library of audio tapes by motivational speakers.

- ○ Create a lending library of books related to your business.

- ○ Contact your association to find books, pamphlets, audio and video tapes, speakers and workshops.

- ○ In large cities, public libraries lend videos and audio tapes, etc.

Examples

Learn It by Teaching

- ○ Staff member demonstrates a new product.

- ○ Two staff members role-play "handling an objection."

- ○ One department demonstrates how to sell their products by selling to another department.

- ○ Demonstrate a new piece of equipment and how to use it.

- ○ Present a new store policy or procedure and explain the reasons behind it.

- ○ Read trade journals, publications and magazines to stay up-to-date. Report to other staff.

- ○ Establish "buddies or trios" to conduct part of the training, encouraging teamwork.

- ○ With a large number of part-timers working different shifts, try bringing them together and have them exchange successes and "near successes" with each other.

- ○ One staff "shadows" another staff for a day and reports what they learned to the group.

- ○ Take a wall of your store, divide it into four sections, ask four people to each merchandise one section and then explain to the rest why they did what they did.

- ○ Have staff demonstrate their specialty in front of the group so others can learn more about speed or accuracy.

- ○ Hand out a work assignment at one meeting and ask staff to complete it and bring it back to the next meeting.

- ○ Send staff to attend trade shows or manufacturers' shows, and ask them to share their learning with others when they return.

Reviews and Quizzes

- ○ End of season quiz: What items are left in stock - size, colour, markdown price?

- ○ Begin the season quiz: What stock do we have today? What is arriving next week? Provide a description, two features, the price and where the items are located in the store.

- ○ Quiz: Is this refund/exchange voucher filled out correctly? If not, correct it.

- ○ Self-assessment - on any job-related subject.

Contests

○ Pair up. The person who can sell the most multiple units to their buddy wins a prize.

○ Bring in one product. Give a prize to the person who can create the largest "go-together" list, to encourage add-on sales. Have them describe why certain items could go together.

○ Walk through the store and notice as many things as you can that are different or new.

Vary the Content

○ Retailers with large numbers of different products in their inventory, that is 5,000 - 7,000 items, spend 90 percent of their training time on product training.

○ Let staff know the "expense" side of your business. They see cash going into the bank continually. When they know what things cost, they are more thrifty and less wasteful.

○ Have a tasting party. Taste your product and compare it to the competition.

○ Provide POS or computer training.

○ Offer presentations on grooming and image.

> *You make time for what is important to you.*

HOW DO SUCCESSFUL RETAILERS FIND THE TIME TO ORGANIZE ALL THE RESOURCES?

○ Some make it a high priority. They take it on as their personal responsibility and they allocate time for it in their schedules.

○ Some use a training committee to develop priorities and plans.

○ Some get together with other merchants in their community and plan joint training sessions, often bringing in outside guests.

○ Some budget 1% of annual gross sales to be set aside for courses and payroll hours; some budget 1.6%[1]

○ All assign some organization and presentation tasks to staff.

Building a learning organization is at the top of the "To Do" list for North America according to the business magazines and business leaders.

> *Coaching and training are as essential as your products!*

[1] *Leadership in Developing the Human Dimension: A Study of Best Practices in Retail and Comparable Companies.* Service Dimensions: Toronto, Ontario. December 1994, page 32.

MEETING PLANNER

Time required	Agenda item	What do you want staff to learn? What do you want to learn?	Method to use	Who to involve

Developing Staff Initiative Through Work Assignment

## 10

This chapter will:

✓ invite you to consider ways to be flexible in your management style

✓ describe how to adapt your management style to different staff

✓ provide questions to help you plan your approach to delegating more to staff

✓ help you to involve staff in planning and decision-making

DEVELOPING STAFF INITIATIVE

Please rate yourself on each of the statements below using the following scale:

1 point = rarely
2 points = some of the time
3 points = most of the time

_____ 1.   My behaviour demonstrates that I am a flexible manager.

_____ 2.   I manage staff in a way that will be most appropriate for them.

_____ 3.   I give staff clear directions when they are working on a new task.

_____ 4.   If a staff person lacks confidence, I offer support.

_____ 5.   If a staff person doesn't understand why some work is required, I take the time to explain the reasons for it.

_____ 6.   I consult with my staff on some important decisions.

_____ 7.   I offer staff who are performing well new challenges and special opportunities to use their knowledge and skills.

_____ 8.   I work with people who are not performing well to make sure they have a chance to improve.

_____ 9.   I look for ways to give staff immediate, accurate feedback on their performance.

_____ 10. I remember that **all** staff need some ongoing support and recognition – no matter the level of their skill and experience.

_____   **TOTAL SCORE**

Interpretation:

10 – 16   You are not providing much direction or support.

17 – 23   You show signs of being a flexible and effective manager.

24 – 30   You take your management responsibilities seriously and probably handle them effectively.

HOW DO YOU GET YOUR STAFF TO TAKE INITIATIVE?

How do you get your staff to take initiative? This question is asked all too often. Some parts of the answer are clear. Staff won't take initiative until you build their competence, confidence and commitment, as well as communicate your trust in them. Chapter 9 describes the coaching and training that provide the foundations for competence and confidence. The early chapters on communication also play essential roles in staff development. This chapter takes you further to show you how to use work assignment to develop initiative and high performance.

Whether or not your staff perform well depends a lot on you and your management style. Do you use a variety of styles or do you use one? Why? Do you believe that you must treat everyone the same?

Do you believe, as some do, that staff should learn how to cope with your style because you are the boss? There is certainly some truth to the notion that staff have to adapt to the style of their boss. However, this is not a sufficient reason for managers to ignore the choices they have in the range of styles they can use. In fact, research shows that when managers match their styles to staff needs, performance improves. Read on to discover what we mean by "management style" and "staff needs."

WHO SHOULD DO WHAT? ASSIGNING THE WORK

Assigning work so that it gets done well is very important and not as easy as it sounds.

The process for assigning work changes from store to store. In small stores with few staff, people often decide together who will do what – receive shipment, cash, etc. In large stores, the manager may take a more active role in co-ordinating staff responsibilities or may delegate the task to people in various departments. While it varies from "we get together and decide among ourselves" to the manager assigning the tasks to be done, it's the manager's role to ensure that the assignment of work is appropriate.

There are many things to consider when work is assigned:

- ○ what needs to be accomplished (i.e. the desired results)
- ○ what tasks need to be done
- ○ the knowledge, skills and experience of your staff
- ○ the level of motivation and self-confidence the staff bring to the particular job.

When you are assigning work, you may tell one staff member only what needs to be accomplished and allow that person to determine the tasks involved and how to do them. In contrast, you may tell another staff member the results you want and specifically how to carry out the tasks required to achieve them. How do you know the level of detail to give to a member of your staff? The situational management model below provides clear guidelines.

SITUATIONAL MANAGEMENT – A HELPFUL MODEL

Two authors named Hershey and Blanchard came up with useful guidelines for managing your staff. They talk about directive management behaviour and supportive management behaviour.

Directive Management Behaviour

Directive management behaviour focuses on expectations for the job. It includes the what, where, when, who and how of the task. The manager focuses on the staff person's **ability to do the job.**

One of the challenges facing a store manager is to decide how much directive behaviour to use. If too little direction is given, misunderstanding may lead to staff frustration, mistakes and waste. If too much direction is given, the staff member may feel "talked down to" and resent the implied lack of confidence. It's the "back seat driver" syndrome: *"Don't tell me what to do! I know how to drive!"*

Your choice of how much directive behaviour to give depends on your assessment of your staff member's ability, as revealed by his or her previous performance, present skills and knowledge.

Supportive Management Behaviour

Supportive management behaviour focuses on helping staff build a positive attitude towards doing the work. It deals with motivation and confidence – factors which influence the staff's **willingness to do the job.**

The manager has choices to make regarding the amount and type of supportive behaviour to offer. If too little support is provided, the staff will not be motivated or may lack self-confidence. If too much is given, it may be experienced as smothering or seen as artificial "hype."

Your choice of how much support to give depends on your assessment of staff's motivation and self-confidence.

> *It has been said that the most unfair thing a manager can do is to treat people who are different in exactly the same manner.*

The Situational Management Model

Every manager's behaviour can be assessed on two dimensions: the amount of direction given for a task, and the amount of support given. If you take opposites on each dimension (high and low), you can describe four major management styles:

THE FOUR LEADERSHIP STYLES

1. **Tell** is high on direction and low on support.

2. **Consult** is high on direction and high support.

3. **Co-operate** is low on direction and high support.

4. **Delegate** is low on both dimensions.

Each of these styles is appropriate under some circumstances. You need to have the **flexibility** to move comfortably from one style to another. You need to know when to use each style.

Before we go on to discuss each of the styles in detail, there are several important things to note:

○ Directive does not mean abrupt, harsh, cold, pushy or anything other than behaviour that is focused on the what, when, how, and where of the task to be done.

○ Supportive does not mean gushy, mushy, coddling or anything other than behaviour that is focused on the feelings and relationships of the person.

○ The model is based on relative emphasis – notice it says "high" and "low," **not** "all" or "nothing." "Low" supportive does not mean ignoring the relationship and motivation; it means less attention is placed on them.

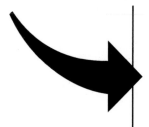

Four Management Styles

Style 1 Tell

This style is high on directive behaviour and low on support. It is needed when a staff person is new. Even an experienced staff person who is new to your store will need to know what, precisely, to do in your store. It is also appropriate when there is a new, challenging task for an experienced staff person. At these times, staff need clear direction. Be very specific about your expectations. Tell people the results you want, what you want them to do and show them how to do it.

Supportive behaviour regarding performance is low (not non-existent, but low) because it is too soon to provide feedback on performance. Of course, you may want to provide encouragement to try things, and express confidence in someone's ability to learn, but put more of your time and effort into giving clear direction.

○ *We need to increase sales by 10 percent this week. We will be making calls to customers about this product. The features are.... The situations in which customers will get good value from using this include.... The major competitive product is.... Its features are....*

AND

This is the way we handle calls to customers. First, we believe the calls are a service to our customers as well as a way to keep us at the top of their minds for hardware goods. So, we start our calls saying something like.... Then we.... If such and such comes up, here is the response I'd like you to use.... Let's practice a call. You play customer and I'll call you, then we'll switch roles.... I'm confident that you'll do this well, especially after a bit of practice.

Style 2 Consult

The second style places an emphasis on both directive behaviour and supportive behaviour. It is called "consult" because the manager acts like a good consultant bringing expertise to the situation (tell) but also observing, listening, and reinforcing the positive things that are already being done (support). This is a very appropriate style to use as a staff person begins to gain some competence with a new task, but still requires direction and encouragement. Your skill in asking questions is useful here. Good consultants ask a lot of questions before giving advice.

○ *Yesterday, we discussed a way to respond to objections the customer may have about this new product. Your ideas were good ones. Since the product will be on special today, I'd like to check out with you how clear I was yesterday. I'd like you to imagine that I'm a customer, I have this product in my hand, and I just said: "This looks different than what I'm used to. I'm concerned it won't work." What would you say to me?*

OR

○ *I am going to put you on cash today. I think you did a good job with new tasks yesterday and you asked thoughtful questions about the cash procedures. So, review for me the steps we went through yesterday.*

Style 3   Co-operate

The third style concentrates on supportive behaviour. It is appropriately applied as the staff gains competence in the "what," "when" and "how" of the task but may still need some encouragement to proceed. As soon as there is good performance to recognize and support, less instruction is needed. When staff reach this competence level, it is discouraging for them to have their manager continue to tell them what to do. Continued direction implies lack of trust. Staff start taking initiative when they have positive feelings about competence and know that management recognizes and appreciates their skill.

The term co-operate suggests a store manager who works along with the staff member, providing little in the way of direct advice, but support and encouragement **as required.**

○ *You are really good at selling our promotions. I particularly like the way you ask the customers questions and then tailor your responses about the features of our promotion to their needs.*

OR

○ *You're making good progress.*

Style 4   Delegate

This style is low on both directive and supportive behaviour. It is appropriate when your staff becomes knowledgeable, skilled and confident about accomplishing their work and are also motivated to do so. You can delegate with little or no worry about the job being done well, because the staff person knows what needs to be done and how to do it. This style is a logical progression from Style 3.

This style could also be called "get out of the way and let staff do what they do well." Here the manager simply stays available, in case he or she is needed, and remembers to say thank-you. This style is what you want to achieve. It gives you more time to pay attention to growing other staff and your business.

○ *Thank you for your initiative in merchandising the front table. It looks good. The contrasting colours and shapes draw attention to our new line. I know I can count on you to make this ... happen. Of course, if you need anything, call me.*

Always Some Support

Think of Carl who is not performing at the expected level. Think of Marnie who is a very independent person who performs well. Remember, both need some contact with you, acknowledgement of their feelings and your respect. How would you deal with Carl? And, what about Marnie? The best matches are Style 1 and Style 4, respectively. Remember:

○ Too Much Direction Produces Dependent, Low Initiative Staff

   How would you feel if someone checked every detail of your work?

   Research has shown that many administrative errors are the result of staff thinking that it is a waste of time to check their work since, regardless of what they do, their bosses will check everything.

○ Too Little Direction Produces Independent Staff Who Make Up the Rules as They Go OR Staff Who Do Not Perform Because They Don't Know What to Do.

The Four Styles Support Natural Stages in Staff Development

Jumping from Style 1 to Style 4 is confusing: "closely supervised one day – abandoned the next." When staff miss the managerial attention of Style 2, they lose important learning as this is the stage in their development when they improve their knowledge and skills. If they miss Style 3, they miss the stage during which they gain your trust in them and build their confidence in themselves.

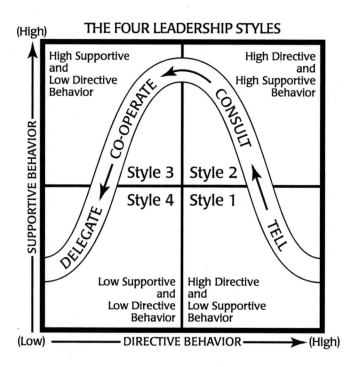

THE FOUR LEADERSHIP STYLES

> **As performance improves, move forward one style (e.g. Style 1 to Style 2).**

> **If performance starts to slip, move back one style (e.g. Style 3 to Style 2).**

People Are Better at Some Tasks than Others

It is possible that a staff person has high competency on some tasks and low competency on others. Joe can need Style 1 management to help him learn how to fit pants, and Style 4 management for calling customers.

Why Work So Hard To Get To Style 4: Delegating?

People use the word "delegating" to mean a variety of behaviours. In this model delegating means giving a person full responsibility for an activity. It is done only when you believe the person has the competence to do the work willingness to do it.

Getting your staff to the stage where they can manage the work with very little direction and support has a number of advantages. It will:

○ create people who can back you up when you are not available

○ add a dimension of reliability that comes from having staff you can count on

○ give you time to do the other important jobs to build your business

○ give you the time you don't have now to coach other staff

○ give you time to check out the competition

○ keep good people challenged and motivated

○ give you time to TAKE A BREAK!

When you delegate, be sure your behaviour supports your staff. If you give a staff person authority to bend store policy, to set a price or to "make a deal" with the customer, don't undermine the authority you have delegated. If a customer asks to see you, the manager, after he or she has been given a price by your staff person, make sure that what you offer is no better a deal than what the staff person offered. If you operate this way, the customer learns to trust the staff and the staff learns to trust you. Doing it any other way only builds up your image, not your business.

Are you as a manager ready to delegate any of your responsibilities? Do you have staff who are ready (competent and willing) to handle delegated responsibilities?

Some managers may not be ready to "let go." Some managers may be ready but may not have staff who are competent. The question for both situations is: How do you ready yourself and your staff?

The following delegation chart will help you sort out your answers to the question.

Questions To Answer	Make the Bank Deposit	Close the Store	Find Three Window Dresser Candidates
DELEGATION PLANNING			
1. Am I ready to delegate this now? (i.e. use Style 4)	Yes	Yes	No
2. What will it take to get me ready?			Involve staff in some interviews with me. Talk about the questions I want to ask and why I want to ask them.
3. a) Is a staff person ready to take this on? If yes, who? If no, move to #4	Selina	Kim	
3. b) What is needed to delegate this?	○ show her how ○ explain the "why" behind the way we do it ○ check her work for two weeks	○ get keys cut ○ tell mall security ○ show Kim how, watch him do it ○ quiz him − what if...?	
3. c) When will I delegate this?	Aug. 31	Aug. 15	
3. d) When will I Check-up, Provide support and Recognition?	Sept. 8	Aug. 16, 18, 22	
4. a) Who could I groom to take on this responsibility? What style does this person need?			Ben needs Style 3 on this task
4. b) What is needed to develop the person?			Provide job description on window dresser, go over questions to ask. How to conduct interviews, get some pictures of sample windows
4. c) Over what time period?			2 months
4. d) When will I delegate this?			Oct. 1
4. e) When will I Check-up, Provide support and Recognition?			

Managing Your Superstars

In his book *Coaching Skills: A Guide for Supervisors,* Robert Lucas offers excellent ideas for working with high performers. First, identify them by their behaviour. They are "superstars" and they:

- Often volunteer for additional assignments

- Exceed deadlines and expectations (in sales and everything else)

- Regularly offer recommendations for improvements

- Help other staff

- Often work in the community (volunteer, special responsibility)

- Test your willingness to give them greater responsibility

When working with superstars, you will realize that you can move through the four situational management styles faster than you can with other staff. They will pick up knowledge and skills faster. **However, they still need guidance and coaching.**

Some high performers need a lot of recognition and appreciation. If their drive to succeed seems based on the need to experience success, they may be eager for learning opportunities, and may want feedback from you on what they are achieving.

Suggestions for coaching the superstar include:

- Give them lots of praise and recognition, publicly and privately.

- Expand their job responsibilities. Ask them to take responsibility for a section of the store, or for special functions like buying, merchandise selection, an industry committee, a merchants' association.

- Help them become coaches, trainers and internal consultants. Suggest they become product experts responsible for sharing knowledge with others. Ask them to review videos, tapes and books and select useful ones for the staff. Ask them to use their skill and experience in orienting new staff.

- Ask for their opinions and advice. Give them research to do (e.g. products, competition).

- Involve them in planning and decision-making.

- Provide personal and professional development activities.

- Talk with them about career opportunities

- Give them opportunities to be highly visible (e.g. on committees, in an article in the newspaper, acting as your representative).

Managing Your "Not-So-Super" Stars

The people who are performing at the low end of the performance scale need to be given special attention as well. For them, the emphasis needs to be on:

○ Setting clear expectations

○ Giving them adequate help to improve

○ Giving them a reasonable amount of time to improve.

Chapter 13, *Dealing with Performance Problems,* and Chapter 14, *Motivation,* provide many more practical strategies for working with these individuals.

It is important to remember that, although other factors come into play, there is a tendency for you to get what you expect, the "self-fulfilling prophecy." Don't label people "low performers," lest the name and the attributions stick. Watch for specific areas in which they are performing well. Give them lots of clear direction and positive support so they can improve. Don't give the challenging assignments to others all the time. Offer them a chance to prove themselves as well. You might be surprised.

GETTING YOUR STAFF INVOLVED IN PLANNING AND DECISION-MAKING

Do you make all the decisions in your store or do you try to involve your staff? It makes good business sense to encourage staff members to become part of the planning and decision-making process because:

○ Retail is getting more complex.

○ You can't know everything and you can't do everything.

○ Staff are better educated than they have ever been before.

○ Involvement in decision-making increases staff awareness of the factors that affect decisions, and their knowledge about the business.

○ People who are involved in making decisions are more committed to them.

○ Your business needs to be able to respond quickly to change.

○ You are wasting your most valuable resources if you don't help staff grow to a stage where they can take on more responsibility.

Some people don't involve their staff in any planning or decision-making because they think it will take too long! Before you say "Wrong!" look at the two diagrams on the next page. The left side of each diagram indicates the time it takes to make a decision. The right side of the diagram, the shaded portion, indicates how long it takes to get that decision fully implemented in your store.

The Authoritarian "Top Down" Approach

Consider Options and Make the Decision	Implement the Decision

Although this top down approach gets a fast decision, the time spent communicating the decision to staff, "selling" them on the idea, explaining how to implement it, and checking up to make sure they have actually done what they were supposed to do takes a long time.

The "Collaborative" Approach

Consider Options and Make the Decision	Implement the Decision

In this second approach, the time spent consulting with staff is much longer. But, once the decision is made, it gets implemented faster because everyone understands the reasons for the decision, the technicalities of implementation, and feels a sense of "ownership" for it. The actual time to full implementation is less than in the first approach.

Better Decisions

Not only will decisions be implemented faster, they will often be better decisions because people worked together, sharing their ideas before they came to a final conclusion.

When To Use a Collaborative Approach

Involving your staff in planning and decision-making has significant benefits. However, there are situations when it doesn't make sense. If the decision isn't very important or if there really aren't any options, don't bother – just go ahead and make the decision on your own. Your staff don't have to be involved in every decision – but when they are, make it count!

SUMMARY

What do we know for sure about planning and assigning responsibilities to our staff? Here are a few key considerations:

1. **Be organized.** Have a plan; know what you want done before you start assigning work to staff.

2. **Consider the capability of your staff members when giving them jobs.** Do they have the knowledge, skills and experience needed? If not, beef up the support they will need to be successful.

3. **Consider their feelings about the assigned work.** Do they have the necessary motivation and self-confidence to do the work? If not, be prepared to be very supportive of them as they take on these assignments.

4. **Consider priorities. Tell staff the most important tasks being assigned.** Have you built in time for them to do the job and the expectation that you will follow up to ensure you're "close to the action" in these areas?

5. **Involve your staff in planning and decision-making about scheduling.** This is an important area that requires the "buy-in" of your staff.

6. **Don't treat everyone the same.** Because people are different, they need to be managed differently. Think about what the staff person needs and be flexible in your management style as you assign work.

Apply the Model

TEST YOUR UNDERSTANDING OF MANAGEMENT STYLES

Imagine that new merchandise has arrived. You want each staff person to call the customers they know as well as ones they don't know. How would you assign this work to:

(a) a staff person who had made calls once or twice before and is willing to make calls again? Which style would you use? Style #_____. What would you say?

(b) a staff person who has had experience, used to hate doing these calls and used to go out of her way to avoid them? Which style would you use? Style #_____. What would you say?

(c) a skillful staff person who has picked up his interest in work after a motivation lull? Which style would you use? Style #_____. What would you say?

(d) a staff person who has demonstrated ability in this area and is self motivated? Which style would you use? Style #_____. What would you say?

(e) a new staff person who would like to avoid making his share of customer calls because he doesn't understand the importance of passing on this information? Which style would you use? Style #_____. What would you say?

(f) a staff person whose telephone skills are not well developed and who avoids making her share of customer calls because she is not motivated about work these days? Which style would you use? Style #_____. What would you say?

(g) a staff person who handles calls fairly well but does not seem confident about them? Which style would you use? Style #_____. What would you say?

The answers follow

ANSWERS FOR "TEST YOUR UNDERSTANDING OF MANAGEMENT STYLES"

Imagine that new merchandise has arrived. You want your staff to call the customers they know as well as ones they don't know. How would you assign this work to:

(a) a staff person who had made calls once or twice before and is willing to make calls again? Which style would you use? Style # _____ . What would you say?

Style 2 – The person has some experience, knows how and is willing.

I think you did a good job with the customer calls you made last month. I'd like to go over planning for this week's calls. How many calls are you planning to make today? What do you want to focus on? What specifically do you think would be best to emphasize with Mary Brown, with George Salmon?... I like the ideas you have. I think your tone is positive. If you need help, don't hesitate to ask.

(b) a staff person who has had experience, used to hate doing these calls and used to go out of her way to avoid them? Which style would you use? Style # _____ . What would you say?

Style 2 – Experienced but unwilling – needs direction and support. If this person were willing, he or she has the experience, and might be a Style 3. Since he or she is unwilling, move back one style to Style 2.

I'd like to understand what makes you want to avoid these calls? What happened when you did them before? What did you call customers about? Role play an old call with me.... I want to know what happened.... In hindsight, how would you handle a customer saying something like that? Here are some other ideas for handling that situation. What else might come up in the calls I am asking you to make? I would like you to let me know what happens in your first five calls. The targets for calls are 20 before Friday. How many can you make before tomorrow night? Good, I'll see you tomorrow, at 6 p.m. after you have made them.

(c) a skillful staff person who has picked up his interest in work after a motivation lull? Which style would you use? Style # _____ . What would you say?

Because the person is skillful, he or she could require only Style 4 management. But the information about "a motivation lull" calls for moving back one "square" to Style 3.

If performance starts to slip, move back one style.

Grow your staff

As performance improves, move forward one style. If performance starts to slip, move back one style.

Good to see your renewed energy. Looking over this list of customers, are there any that you would like to discuss before you call? Let me know how they are going.

(d) a staff person who has demonstrated ability in this area and is self-motivated? Which style would you use? Style # _____. What would you say?

Style 4.

Is there anything you need regarding the sales calls?

(e) new staff who would like to avoid making their share of customer calls because they don't understand the importance of passing on this information? Which style would you use? Style # _____. What would you say?

Style 1.

I think that you might not consider calling customers worth the effort. Perhaps this was your experience at your last job? Have you ever been called by a store as one of their customers? What did you think? How could that call have been better?

We track our figures before and after we make calls. I have a bit of an analysis here. The last time we made customer calls, our figures for the week before we made them were... for the week we made them were... and for the next two weeks after were....
We also have figures from last season.

Now, I want to go over with you how we do customer calls here. We start off by saying something like... then.... If the customer says... I think a good answer would be.... If a customer asks about... you might respond by.... I'd like you also to ask the customer how he/she feels about being called like this, and write down what they say. OK? Let's try out a couple of calls. I'll be you and you act as a customer, then we'll reverse roles.

(f) a staff person whose telephone skills are not well developed and who avoid making their share of customer calls because they are not motivated about work these days? Which style would you use? Style # _____. What would you say?

Style 1 because skills and motivation are low.

Yesterday, we talked about motivation and that there are normal cycles of moving from higher to lower levels and back up..... I know you are not feeling at the top of yours. We need to call our customers and I want to make sure you will convey an upbeat note. I'd like you to talk about. ... If the customer asks about... you might respond by.... Let's try out a couple of calls. I'll be you and you act as a customer then we'll reverse roles. Given the traffic and lack of shipments today, I think somewhere between 10 and 15 calls is a fair target. You can start in half an hour – John should be finished with the phone by then.

(g) a staff person who handles calls fairly well but does not seem confident about them? Which style would you use? Style # _____. What would you say?

Style 3 – Skill is good and so is willingness. He or she needs encouragement and positive feedback.

You did a good job with the calls last month. I think your approach of referring back to the last time the customer was in the store was effective. It's important to keep our name in their minds and you are a good ambassador for us.

Help staff reach their full potential

MANAGEMENT STYLE PLANNING SHEET

Use the planning guide below to summarize the appropriate management style for each staff person in relation to the major tasks they are asked to do. List your staff down the left side. Beside each staff person, identify 2 or 3 specific tasks. Note your thoughts on the management style the person needs on each task. A staff person might need different management styles on different types of work. In the last column, write down comments you might use. A blank form is provided at the end of the chapter.

Staff Member	Type Of Task	Management Style	What You Might Say
Jamal	Customer Service ○ ordinary sales ○ handling returns	Style 4 – Delegate Style 3 – Co-operate	*Let me know if you need anything* *You handled the last return well. Any questions?*
Karen	Customer Service ○ handling problems with customers Sales ○ new cash out system	Style 2 – Consult Style 1 – Tell	*Let's review the conversation you had with the customer who said that parts were missing out of the box...* *Here the purpose of the new cash out system is ....* *It's designed so that....* *The steps are....* *Let's try it out.*

MANAGEMENT STYLE PLANNING SHEET

Staff Member	Type Of Task	Management Style	What You Might Say

DELEGATION PLANNING

Questions To Answer	Activities or Tasks		
1. Am I ready to delegate this now? (i.e. use Style 4)			
2. What will it take to get me ready?			
3. a) Is a staff person ready to take this on? If yes, who? If no, move to #4			
3. b) What is needed to delegate this?			
3. c) When will I delegate this?			
3. d) When will I Check-up, Provide support and Recognition?			
4. a) Who could I groom to take on this responsibility? What style does this person need?			
4. b) What is needed to develop the person?			
4. c) Over what time period?			
4. d) When will I delegate this?			
4. e) When will I Check-up, Provide support and Recognition?			

Recognizing and Rewarding Staff

## 11

This chapter will:

✓ describe two types of recognition

✓ discuss questions that must be answered to develop an overall approach to formal rewards and recognition

✓ walk you through eight steps to plan and implement a specific reward program

✓ provide examples of rewards used by successful retailers

REWARDS AND RECOGNITION

How well are you managing the rewards and recognition in your store? Use the following rating scale to help you decide:

0 points = not relevant to me and my store
1 point = this needs much more attention
2 points = doing this OK
3 points = doing this well

_____ 1. I consistently acknowledge staff for their efforts and results.

_____ 2. When mistakes are made as staff struggle to learn something new, I recognize the effort and the desire to learn.

_____ 3. I look for new ways to provide rewards and recognition.

_____ 4. I look for new ways to provide increased responsibility for staff.

_____ 5. I ask staff for their opinions and follow up on them.

_____ 6. Formal rewards are planned and carefully timed to maintain motivation over the year.

_____ 7. I use rewards to serve different purposes – acknowledge outstanding performance, build teamwork, reinforce new habits, etc.

_____ 8. The specific results, and the activities and behaviours required to be eligible for a reward are clearly identified.

_____ 9. Staff in my store feel valued or appreciated for the work they do.

_____ 10. The winners of contests or promotions are communicated to the rest of the staff.

_____ 11. Rewards are available for the achievement of challenging but possible results.

_____ 12. Rewards acknowledge the non-selling roles that support sales.

_____ **TOTAL SCORE**

Interpretation

0 – 12   You are missing the positive impact of rewards and recognition on staff performance.

13 – 20   You have a commitment to recognizing your staff. There is information in this chapter to move you forward.

21 – 28   You are on a useful path. This chapter will reinforce what you are doing and offer some new ideas.

29 – 36   Congratulations. Keep up the good work.

WHY OFFER REWARDS?

Why should you reward staff for doing the job you pay them to do? Retailers answered:

- ○ *We expect a lot from our staff, sometimes more than we should.*

- ○ *Even when you are expected to do a job, and you agree to do it, you like your work to be appreciated.*

- ○ *I've learned that a pen or a plaque goes a long way towards encouraging staff to go that extra mile.*

- ○ *It doesn't cost very much to find different ways of saying thank-you.*

- ○ *An investment in an incentive or perk is an investment in the growth of my business.*

TYPES OF REWARDS AND RECOGNITION

There are many types of recognition. For ease of discussion we are dividing them into two categories:

1. Habitual Acknowledgment

2. Planned Recognition and Reward Programs

Habitual Acknowledgement

People feel recognized and valued when you:

- ○ acknowledge their uniqueness

- ○ ask for their ideas

- ○ provide feedback on their ideas

- ○ recognize, in public, the good job they have done

- ○ offer increased responsibility.

Make it a habit to notice and acknowledge your staff on a daily basis. Nothing can replace the variety of behaviours that regularly tell staff: "I see you. I value you." These behaviours cost nothing and yield high returns. In some ways, these behaviours are really no more than common courtesy.

- ○ Nice hair cut, it looks good on you!

- ○ Enjoy your lunch, the back room looks terrific.

- ○ Thanks for your patience teaching Mary the paperwork again today.

- ○ How is your daughter progressing in her course?

It's human nature to want to be noticed and recognized.

Giving recognition is a personal discipline.

People feel valued when you ask for their opinion. Of course, it's essential to follow up. Respond to suggestions by providing feedback on the pros and cons as you see them, what you would like to do, and what you will do. If you are going to use or adapt an idea, indicate the timing.

- ○ *I'm interested in your opinion, how do you think we could:*
    - ○ *Improve the window treatment?*
    - ○ *Be better prepared for the markdowns?*
    - ○ *Organize the stock- room?*
    - ○ *Make the cash desk more efficient?*
- ○ *I would appreciate it if you would give it some thought.*

It doesn't take much time to draw attention, in a positive way, to what a staff member or a team has done. Comments like the ones below show that you notice and appreciate staff. The comments motivate continued performance, and build loyalty to a boss who cares.

- ○ *Linda, Mr. Skenner told me how much he appreciated the special order you got him.*
- ○ *Have you seen the great job Jim did in the back room? Go and look.*
- ○ *I'm glad you dropped into the store. It gives me a chance to tell you that your son made three customers very happy today and I'm pleased he's on our team.*
- ○ *Let's have a round of applause for Sharon. We love the assortment you bought.*
- ○ On a bulletin board: *Congratulations to Steve for locating the lost goods.*
- ○ *Let's have a team cheer for everyone's efforts on the markdown program.*
- ○ *The team player is Alphonse for learning our new inventory system so fast and helping the rest of us when we forget.*

Planned Recognition and Reward Systems

Recognition and reward programs are tools you can use to support sales and service. Many retailers don't have a formal program. Some give a bonus or gift at Christmas or another special time of year. If this works for you and your staff, perhaps you do not need to develop anything more complicated. However, there are many retailers who will tell you that a planned approach to rewards is a powerful tool in sales, customer service and team building. A planned approach answers the following questions:

❍ What reward should I give to which staff person and for what reason?

❍ How often should I provide formal rewards?

❍ How can I ensure that I am being perceived as fair?

❍ How can I relate rewards to store goals and values, as well as to the motivation of my staff?

PLANNING YOUR OVER-ALL APPROACH

The answers to the following five questions will help you plan your overall approach to rewards and formal recognition.

1. What purposes do you want to achieve through your recognition and reward programs?

2. How much you will invest in a rewards and recognition program for your staff?

3. How will you allocate your rewards and recognition budget across the purposes you want to achieve?

4. What types of programs have you used in the past? What types are you thinking of using?

5. How will you spread the different programs over the year?

THE AIM

THE BUDGET

THE PLAN

THE TOOLS

THE TIMING

When you answer the fifth question, you will be able to see a year's worth of recognition and reward programs. At a glance, you will be able to check whether your distribution of rewards reflects what you value. You will be ready to plan the details of the individual programs. First, let's look at each question.

1. What purposes do you want to achieve through recognition and reward programs?

Overall Approach – THE AIM

Before developing a particular recognition and reward program, consider what you want to accomplish throughout the year. The following six outcomes illustrate commonly desired results. Many start with the words "stimulate and acknowledge" to remind us that the possibility of rewards can be motivating for people who are energized by achievement and recognition needs.

You will return to the following purposes many times as you plan:

○ **Stimulate and acknowledge outstanding performance**

Performance can mean results only or it can include both the results and how they were achieved (activities, and the behaviours used to achieve them). This could apply to any aspect of any job. In sales, performance might mean sales productivity, customer service activities and compliance with guidelines for customer service. In administration, it might refer to receiving, shipping, scheduling and cost containment. In buying, it might mean sales targets and inventory turns.

○ **Stimulate and improve performance**

This type of purpose is set apart from the one above to allow for the staff person who may not be able to produce results at the "outstanding level," yet, but has significantly improved behaviour and results. This may apply to a new hire, to someone working in a new position, to someone recovering from an illness, etc.

○ **Reinforce new patterns of behaviour**

What might be "new patterns of behaviour"? Perhaps you have introduced a new approach to customer service that requires a change in behaviour. Perhaps you have instituted a new record keeping system that staff have had trouble remembering to use. Perhaps you want to stimulate more teamwork. Perhaps you want to institute a particular cost containment approach.

○ **Increase the inventory turns, sell specific types of merchandise**

You may ask your buyer to source a product that will be hard to find or challenging to buy with your budget. You may ask your staff to focus on certain products to improve inventory turnover.

○ **Develop and recognize loyalty**

Perhaps you want to create ways of recognizing behaviours that demonstrate loyalty in ways that you value.

○ **Develop and maintain teamwork**

Recognizing the importance of co-operation and collaboration, you may want to promote teamwork by rewarding it.

2. How much will you invest in a rewards and recognition program for your staff.

Some retailers allocate a percentage of revenues to employee reward programs. Others base their budgets on an average amount they want to spend per employee. A dollar a month? Five dollars a month? Ten dollars? Whatever figure you come to, multiply it by the number of employees you want to reward and you will have your overall budget. Some retailers want to formally reward every employee in some way. Others decide that they want to reward only a portion of their staff. This depends on the purposes they want to achieve through their reward programs and their personal beliefs about rewarding people.

In The Greatest Management Principle, *Michael Le Boeuf says that organizations seldom reward the behaviour they value and that managers seldom use all the rewards at their disposal.*

Overall Approach – THE BUDGET

DEVELOPING HIGH PERFORMING STAFF

The budget will vary from store to store. Don't be discouraged if your profits limit your budget to a relatively small amount. There are many inexpensive ways to express recognition. The list on page 186 offers many ideas.

What do you do if you have many staff to reward? First, celebrate their skills and your ability to draw out their performance potential. Second, re-examine your budget to see whether you are allocating as much as you possibly can to acknowledge people's contributions. Third, if your budget is still less than you need, consider two-level reward programs. That is, anyone who qualifies for the reward (i.e. meets the criteria) becomes eligible to win. From among all the people who are eligible, draw one or more winners.

3. How will you spread your rewards and recognition budget across the purposes you want to achieve?

Overall Approach – THE PLAN

Take the budget that you developed in response to question 2, and ask yourself what percent you want to allocate to each of your purposes. Ask yourself:

○ Do I want to spread it evenly across all the purposes I want to achieve?

○ Do I want to emphasize a few purposes? Which ones?

Once you have indicated the percentage you want to allocate to each purpose, translate that into the dollars available for each purpose. That will be the amount you have to spend for as many programs as you want for that one purpose. For example, you may decide to allocate 25 percent of your rewards and recognition budget to developing and maintaining teamwork. If your budget was $1000, you would have $250 to spend on different ways to reward teams. You might spend the $250 on one reward or allocate it among several programs over the year.

4. What types of rewards do you want to use? What have you used in the past? What types are you thinking of using?

Overall Approach – THE TOOLS

In 1991, *The Service Edge and Total Quality* newsletters, in conjunction with Maritz Inc., experts in performance improvement systems, surveyed companies regarding service quality incentives. Over 90 firms responded to a question about what they gave winners. Many firms offer a combination of cash, merchandise and symbolic rewards.

○ 46 per cent mentioned cash rewards

○ 46 per cent mentioned merchandise

○ 54 per cent mentioned symbolic rewards.

What types of rewards have you used in the past? Were they received well? Did they serve your purposes? Consider other types of reward programs (e.g. bonuses, incentives, contests, etc) including the ones on page 186. Then, list the types of rewards that might be suitable for your purposes and budget on a chart like the one that follows as a way to begin developing an overall plan.

OVERALL APPROACH TO REWARDS AND RECOGNITION

Budget for this year:

Purpose of the Reward	% of the recognition and rewards budget allocated to this purpose	Dollars allocated to this purpose	List of the types of rewards that might be suitable for this purpose? (possibilities)	What is the best timing for these rewards?
Stimulate and acknowledge outstanding performance				
Stimulate and improve performance				
Reinforce new patterns of behaviour				
Increase the inventory, or sell specific types of merchandise				
Develop and recognize loyalty				
Develop and maintain teamwork				

Overall Approach – THE TIMING

As you think about the opportunities and constraints, and as you weigh different types of rewards, costs, and budget, your first estimates might need revision. Thinking about an overall approach involves moving back and forth between these possibilities.

5. How will you spread the different programs over the year?

Spread out a sheet of paper that shows fifty-two weeks. Consider the buying, inventory and sales cycles, and ask yourself:

 ○ when do people need some excitement or a motivational boost?

 ○ when will each different reward best achieve your purposes?

Momentum generated by special events will not last for extended periods of time. Specific events could last a day, a week, a month, or a season. Few extend for a year.

Mark each reward you are considering on a post-it note or coloured strip of paper. Move them around so that you have the balance you want across the year. Then identify a starting and closing week for each reward program. This will give you a guide for the detail planning of each program.

PURPOSES	REWARD PROGRAMS	WEEKS 1-4				WEEKS 5-8				WEEKS 9-12				WEEKS 13-16				WEEKS 17-20				WEEKS 21-24				WEEKS 25-28				WEEKS con't...			
		1	2	3	4	5	6	7	8	9	10	11	12	13	14	15	16	17	18	19	20	21	22	23	24	25	26	27	28	29	30	31	32
Develop & Maintain Teamwork	○ Night at Theatre ○ Best Team Results Bonus					x								x	x	x	x																
Reinforce New Patterns of Behavior	Customer Survey Filled In? You Can Win																																

The use of these planning charts will help you think about your options for an overall program. You will find that you change the timing or the type of reward several times until you have the overall approach that best meets your purposes, the buying and selling cycles, and the motivation needs of your staff.

Full chart on page 189.

INVOLVE YOUR STAFF

Asking staff for their ideas is a powerful form of recognition. It can also tailor your program to staff preferences. Use a regular staff meeting or call a special one to share your purposes and invite suggestions for types of rewards for each of your purposes. Then share your thinking regarding the types of different reward programs you have in mind and the timing of them.

PLANNING AND IMPLEMENTING A SPECIFIC REWARD PROGRAM

For planning and implementing a reward program related to a specific purpose, there are seven steps:

Make people who work for you feel important. If you honour and serve them, they'll honour and serve you.

1. Review the purpose.

2. Identify what you want to reward (i.e., the specific behaviours, activities and results) and how you will identify winners.

3. Decide on the reward to be given.

4. Decide how long the program will last.

5. Clearly communicate what staff need to do (the behaviours and results you expect) to be eligible for a reward.

6. Monitor and measure the activities or behaviours you want to reward.

7. Distribute the rewards and announce the winners to your staff.

8. Assess the success of the program.

1. **Review your purposes.**

Review the purposes for the specific program you will be planning.

2. **Identify what you want to reward (the specific behaviours, activities and results) and how you will identify winners.**

The purposes you identified in Step 1 must be translated into what a staff person or team must achieve (results) and/or must do (behaviours, activities) to be rewarded.

You must also decide who will qualify for the reward. How will you know when someone is eligible to win? Will you measure and track results and behaviour? Will you use managerial discretion? Will you ask staff and/or customers to nominate winners?

As you will see from the examples below, this is not as complicated as it sounds.

○ **Purpose: stimulate and acknowledge outstanding performance.** What will count as "outstanding" performance? What can you measure? Note that it is motivating to be asked to meet a challenge that is both difficult and possible.

Sales per hour? Sales per week? Outstanding could be a specified percentage above the store average or a defined increase in sales over last year. Outstanding could be defined as cost savings of a certain number of dollars or a percentage of costs.

"Going the extra mile" in any job function could be defined by staff as another indicator of outstanding performance.

○ A bookstore and coffee shop use similar systems. They both set goals for hourly sales. They assess the success of a shift by the average sales each hour. Because of the nature of their business, they can't recognize one individual. They reward all the staff who work on the shift that exceeds the goals by a specified amount.

○ A store with three departments sets department goals on a daily basis and tracks individual sales performance as well. When goals are exceeded, they reward both the entire department and also the outstanding individual contributors.

○ Several stores hire "mystery shoppers" who comment on the customer service and sales approach of the staff. According to criteria staff develop with the owner, the mystery shopper fills out a checklist about behaviours that are relevant and exhibited during the visit to the store. Each staff person gets personalized feedback. Staff who are rated at the excellent level a certain number of times receive a reward. A variation of this idea is to have mystery shoppers allocate points based on their shopping experience. Rewards would be given to the person or team with the most points.

○ **Purpose: stimulate and improve performance.** What will count as an improvement? How will you know there has been one? What will you need to see and hear to believe that performance has improved?

○ **Purpose: reinforce new patterns of behaviour.** What are the new behaviour patterns that you want to reinforce?

Perhaps you asked your customers what they value about your store and what they wish you would do. Perhaps you have developed a list of things staff can do to meet what customers want.

Perhaps you want to focus on handling inventory differently. Perhaps you want to reduce the time required to get merchandise on the floor, or you want to reduce breakage.

○ **Purpose: increase the inventory turns (for a buyer), or sell specific types of merchandise (for sales staff).** How much will count as an increase worthy of recognition? How many units do you want bought or sold?

○ **Purpose: develop and recognize loyalty.** How is loyalty demonstrated and what specifically do you want to reward?

In stores where there is a large staff turnover within six months, loyalty might mean a reward after eight months. If turnover is a pattern you do not want, examine closely what is causing it. Are you hiring the wrong people? Is the orientation inadequate? Is the job poorly designed? Is there too little recognition to sustain the challenges? Is the store climate (both physical and psychological) poor? Is there too much conflict? Is the problem with the boss? And so on.

What about acknowledging anniversaries after a number of years of service? Honouring someone's ongoing commitment is important and can provide an opportunity to build team spirit. However, this should not be the only form of recognition you offer.

Loyalty can also be an act of courage or wisdom that protects the store, its image, its reputation, and its owner and staff.

Identify what you want to reward.

Everyone is a potential winner. Some people are disguised as losers; don't let their appearances fool you.

Ken Blanchard

○ **Purpose: promote and maintain teamwork.** For what kind of behaviour should a team be rewarded?

Could team performance be defined in ways similar to the definitions offered above for individual performance (e.g. the team with the highest sales over store average, or the best sales over target)?

How about contribution to the team? What individual behaviours should be rewarded? Ask your staff. It is important that they have input to defining this category.

Store goals and store values must be considered before you finalize the results, activities and behaviours required for a reward. If the store goals are to make a certain level of profit, then achieving sales results should not be accomplished at the expense of profit. For example, the results achieved by offering tailoring service that eats into the profit should not be rewarded. If your store values teamwork, then sales results achieved by a team member who "hogs" the sales should not be rewarded. If customer service is achieved but staff have been rude and nasty to each other in the process, the reward should not be given.

Ask staff to comment on the results, activities and behaviours that you have defined as the criteria for eligibility for the reward. Are they challenging? Possible? Fair?

3. Decide on the reward to be given.

When you planned your overall approach, you estimated the amount of money available. Consider the ideas you had at that time and decide on the type of reward you will use.

Although staff like to receive tangible rewards; they highly value the fact that you are providing a reward. As you can see in the list on page 186, rewards can be simple or elaborate, monetary or symbolic, low or high in cost. When you plan the reward, think about matching the reward to the person. If you allocate $20, consider spending it on a CD for the music lover or on a restaurant voucher for a person who likes to eat in restaurants.

- ○ A store that requires staff to wear its product, sells it to them at cost plus 20 per cent. It offers a reward system to help staff get more clothing. To encourage staff to sell specific products, one per cent of the sales price, over a certain dollar amount, is allocated towards the purchase of more clothing in the store. Staff are eligible after their daily sales target is met. Because staff love the merchandise, this reward program works really well for them.

- ○ *Achieving Customer Loyalty* by Marilyn Currie reports on the system used at Simek's Meat and Seafood Store in Minneapolis/St.Paul. Any employee who delivers exceptional service is rewarded with a certificate for an extra hour's worth of pay. The manager gives a certificate when he or she sees an employee going the extra mile, like a stock person seen delivering a cart to a customer who was carrying an armful of groceries. Positive comments from customers also lead to rewards.

- ○ Several companies encourage staff to say "thank you" to colleagues in the company. A thank you note describes the deed done and its impact. After receiving a number of cards, the recipient is rewarded with a choice of gifts, all worth a similar amount.

4. Decide how long the program will last.

When you planned your overall approach, you had an idea for the timing of this particular reward program. You may need to fine-tune the starting and closing dates.

5. Communicate with staff.

Present each reward program with excitement and energy. Be clear about what is expected. Share decisions you made in Steps 2, 3 and 4. Raise the energy by talking up the event and the reward.

6. Monitor and measure the results, activities or behaviours required for the reward.

Tracking sales is not difficult. Measuring and monitoring customer service is more difficult. But it can be done and it is worth the effort. Many retailers use mystery shoppers and customer comment cards. *Achieving Customer Loyalty* by Marilyn Currie offers additional ideas.

○ When a customer compliments a salesperson, the retailer puts the name in a large glass jar. Once a season, three names are drawn for rewards, and the rest of the names are posted on the bulletin board with a thank you note from the owner.

○ One retailer provided gift baskets for a contest that lasted two weeks and was associated with a theme event. The salesperson wrote his or her name on part of the sales ticket for every item sold during the two-week period. The part with the salesperson's name was put into an envelope. The more staff sold, the more times their name went into the envelope and the greater their chances of winning. Draws for three winners were made one week after the event. The delay kept up the suspense and speculation about who would win.

7. Reward the staff who met the expectations and communicate their achievements to the rest of your team.

Give some thought to how you will announce and congratulate the winners. The predictability of having a regular time and place for announcement of rewards is an advantage that allows part-timers to call in to find out results. Varying the timing and method of announcements allows you to increase the suspense and be more creative. Try both. One retailer occasionally has a balloon company or florist deliver the announcement. Another has used a "cookie-gram."

8. Assess the success of the program.

In your view, was it successful? Did it achieve the purpose you hoped it would in Step 1 when you were planning it? Did it have any other positive results? Were there results that you do not want (e.g. neglect of duties other than the ones being rewarded, conflict between staff)? And what do store sales and service reports indicate?

Planning a Specific Reward Program
Step 4

Step 5

Step 6

Step 7

Step 8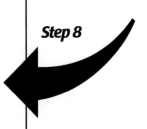

What do staff say about the program? Invite their comments; they know how they feel about the process and the results.

The rest of the chapter will provide ideas that are being used successfully by retailers. Notice the number of low cost ones.

TYPES OF REWARDS USED BY SUCCESSFUL RETAILERS

Examples

- ◯ Extra discounts on merchandise

- ◯ Symbolic gifts (candles with a note "you light up this place"; a banana for being the top banana; "hour off" chits that can be accumulated for up to one day off and claimed on week days; a button with an appropriate saying, etc.)

- ◯ T- shirts: "WE DID IT!" "WE ARE THE CHAMPIONS" for your staff; "My Dad/Mom is great" for their children; "I love my granddad/grandmom and so does Jordan Hardware" for grandchildren of staff.

- ◯ Personalized coffee mug, card, T-shirt, tote bag, pen, etc.

- ◯ Trade products (or gift certificates for your products) with local retailers for use as gifts

- ◯ Group activities (baseball, bowling, picnic, theatre, party)

- ◯ A title for a month or a year: Editor of Newsletter, Director of Inventory, Visual Creator of Windows

- ◯ Vouchers (for CDs and audio tapes, for software, for restaurants) and tickets (for movies, theatre, sporting events, ski passes, etc.)

- ◯ Monthly memo from the owner – outlines successes and future plans

- ◯ Charts, in the back room, displaying individual performance, shift performance and total store performance. Coloured markers or balloons highlight the achievers.

- ◯ A special parking space for a week, month or year

- ◯ Once-a-year recognition in a local newspaper

- ◯ A call or letter from the owner

- ◯ Being sent to a conference

- ◯ An invitation to represent the store on an Association committee

- ◯ Newspaper clipping: "Basic Books thanks their staff Mary Rouc, Janet Touri, Arturo Ganbera, Marg Fenton for their commitment to knowing all about the products you, our customers want, and for their dedication to meeting your needs."

YOU HAVE WINNERS – REWARD THEM

Does your store have a couple of superstars who are likely to win all the time? They always have the highest sales, the most items on a sale, and their targets met. While it is important to rewards your superstars, it's also important to make sure that other staff are recognized too. Sourcing products, store administration, store maintenance – a lot of behind-the-scenes work goes into a sale.

A thank-you is always appreciated. There are so many ways to say it. Ask your staff for ideas. Talk to other retailers. Use your creativity. Experiment. Staff will appreciate your efforts.

ACTION PLANNING

What ideas do you want to remember	Page #	When and How Do You Want to Implement Them	Who Can Help You?	By When?
_____	_____	_____	_____	_____
_____	_____	_____	_____	_____
_____	_____	_____	_____	_____
_____	_____	_____	_____	_____
_____	_____	_____	_____	_____
_____	_____	_____	_____	_____
_____	_____	_____	_____	_____
_____	_____	_____	_____	_____
_____	_____	_____	_____	_____
_____	_____	_____	_____	_____
_____	_____	_____	_____	_____
_____	_____	_____	_____	_____
_____	_____	_____	_____	_____
_____	_____	_____	_____	_____
_____	_____	_____	_____	_____
_____	_____	_____	_____	_____
_____	_____	_____	_____	_____
_____	_____	_____	_____	_____
_____	_____	_____	_____	_____
_____	_____	_____	_____	_____
_____	_____	_____	_____	_____

OVERALL APPROACH TO REWARDS AND RECOGNITION

Budget for this year:

Purpose of the Reward	% of the rewards budget allocated to this award	Dollars allocated to this award	What types of rewards might be suitable for this purpose?	What is the best timing for these rewards?

OVERALL APPROACH

	WEEKS 1-4	WEEKS 5-8	WEEKS 9-12	WEEKS 13-16	WEEKS 17-20	WEEKS 21-24	WEEKS 25-28	WEEKS 29-32	WEEKS 33-36	WEEKS 37-40	WEEKS 41-44	WEEKS 45-48	WEEKS 49-52
	1 2 3 4	5 6 7 8	9 10 11 12	13 14 15 16	17 18 19 20	21 22 23 24	25 26 27 28	29 30 31 32	33 34 35 36	37 38 39 40	41 42 43 44	45 46 47 48	49 50 51 52
REWARD PROGRAMS													
PURPOSES													

REWARD PROGRAM

Name of Reward:

Dollars Available:

Start Date: **End Date:**

Reward is for   ❑ **Individuals**   ❑ **Team**   ❑ **Both**

The reward will be:	The value of each reward will be:
Results and behaviour required to be eligible	How will these results be measured?
Activities and behaviours required	How will these activities and behaviours be measured?
How many winners will there be?	How will reward winners be chosen from eligible successful staff?
How will reward winners find out they won? How will all staff receive the news?	How will others who were eligible be congratulated for qualifying and informed of the winners?

Reviewing Performance With Staff

This chapter will:

✓ outline the benefits of reviewing performance with your staff

✓ define a performance review process

✓ outline ten steps in a performance review process

✓ describe how to prepare yourself and your staff for a review conversation

✓ discuss common pitfalls and ways to avoid them

✓ provide sample forms to use in a review

## 12

REVIEWING STAFF PERFORMANCE

Use the following rating scale to help you decide how frequently you do the following:

1 point = rarely
2 points = sometimes
3 points = very often

_____ 1. I tell staff up front that I will be reviewing their performance with them on a regular basis.

_____ 2. I ensure there are no surprises at performance review time.

_____ 3. I take time to prepare myself for the discussion with each staff person.

_____ 4. I ask staff to come prepared to discuss their thoughts on their performance.

_____ 5. I schedule time and a location where we will not be interrupted.

_____ 6. I begin the discussion by setting a positive tone.

_____ 7. I start by discussing a strength or an accomplishment.

_____ 8. I encourage an open discussion between us.

_____ 9. I ask what they have learned and what they would change in the future.

_____ 10. I ask what obstacles get in the way of their achieving high performance.

_____ 11. I offer suggestions and listen to their suggestions.

_____ 12. I set future goals with staff and clarify our agreements.

_____ 13. I end the discussion by offering encouragement and confidence in their abilities.

_____ 14. I ask what help they need from me.

_____ 15. I thank them for their time and contribution.

_____ **TOTAL SCORE**

Interpretation:

15 – 25   There will be a positive surprise for you when you implement the ideas in this chapter.

26 – 35   You are on your way to conducting effective performance reviews and will find tips here to assist you.

36 – 45   You are doing a fine job with staff reviews.

REVIEWING YOUR ASSETS

You review your sales and revenue each season. You review the merchandise and inventory. In the same way, it's useful to review staff performance.

You invest a lot of time and effort in selecting and hiring staff. It's important to continue investing after the staff member starts work. Did you choose wisely? You can't tell after one day on the job. It takes time.

Even after a staff member has been on staff for a long time, it is helpful to continue some form of assessment. New products, different customers, and new market conditions may change your staffing needs. Some staff members will grow with the business. Others may get left behind.

WHAT IS A PERFORMANCE REVIEW?

A review is a discussion about how a staff person has performed over a period of time. It focuses on performance relative to expectations, the job description and the past and future goals of both the manager and the staff person. Reviews are not one-way evaluations. They are an exchange of perceptions and expectations.

Periodic performance reviews are part of coaching but they are also different from it. On a daily basis, staff get "snapshots" of their performance through your coaching and feedback. They don't get your view of the whole "movie" of their performance. You need to complete the "big picture" from time to time.

In the sample of high-performing retailers, some do staff performance reviews seasonally; some do them biannually; some do them once a year; and a few don't do them at all. The ones who do not do them at all are the ones who have daily and weekly coaching conversations. All the retailers in our high-performing sample, and all the retailers you read about in magazines, give their staff feedback and coaching.

WHY BOTHER REVIEWING PERFORMANCE?

Through periodic reviews you can:

- ○ identify top-notch performance and encourage more of it

- ○ reward the performance you expect and send very clear messages about what will be expected in the future

- ○ identify problem areas that need attention and do something about them **now.** This will prevent them from happening over and over again

- ○ save yourself time and frustration

- ○ build staff morale and a strong sales team.

Performance reviews can be living proof of how important staff are to you.

an open discussion between two people both concerned with future success – a partnership

Why do we have special days like birthdays, anniversaries, Mother's Day, and so on, throughout the year? They are not simply creations of retailers to stimulate sales. They meet our need to recognize and appreciate others. In the spirit of such days, a performance review can perform the same function in your work setting – letting people know that you are aware of what they do, and that you appreciate their efforts. The review that is handled well can leave people feeling more enthusiastic about their work and clearer about ways to improve.

Reviews can be one of the most effective ways to provide your staff with **living proof** of how important their role is. It's important enough for you to make time to talk. For most retailers, it's important enough to pay for the staff time involved in the review. Some managers have developed such trust, respect and open communication with staff that they find the process quite enjoyable and easy. Some keep a written record of the discussions. Others don't feel the need to do so.

A standard performance review form that reflects the job duties and the values of the store can be quite useful to clarify and reinforce expectations, as well as to record information for future action. Samples are provided on pages 204 – 207.

STAFF PERFORMANCE IS REALLY A REFLECTION OF YOU!

See also Chapters 9 and 10

1. If you find that each of your staff members is performing well in all areas of the job, you have probably hired the right people and trained and coached them very well. Reviews are an opportunity to give them the positive recognition and support they deserve. Since there is a temptation to give less attention to people who are performing well, the review helps you maintain contact to ensure the staff will continue to be highly effective.

2. If you find that each staff member is performing well in some areas of the job, but not in others, you have probably hired the right person, but have more training and coaching to do. Use reviews to set performance goals and to identify the support needed for these improvements.

3. If you find that a staff member is not performing well in many areas of the job, you may have hired the wrong person for the job or not provided the training or coaching that was needed. Use reviews to identify the particular problem areas and to set goals for improvement. The process may also provide information about what went wrong in your hiring process. If all else fails, it will provide documentation for dismissal.

How Well Have You Been Performing?

See also Chapter 13

How many staff do you have that fit in Category #1 above? Category #2? Category #3?

TEN STEPS TO A SUCCESSFUL PERFORMANCE REVIEW

The ten steps below will help you ensure that every review is a positive and worthwhile experience for both the staff member and you.

1. Take Time to Prepare

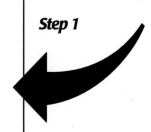

Step 1

Take the time needed to prepare your thoughts and your comments before you meet the staff member. What have you asked this person to do during the period under review? What has been the level of performance? What do you appreciate most about this person? What improvements are needed? Decide if you wish to use any particular forms or models as part of the process. (See pages 204 – 207 for some examples.)

Think about the performance expectations you have had for the store and this person. If expectations have been met, do you "raise the bar" or leave it as is? If expectations have not been met, do you want to "lower the bar" or leave it as is?

In relation to the person with whom you'll be talking, you will need real life examples that are specific to illustrate the points you want to make. To select these examples, review the entire period, not just the last few days or weeks. Decide what behaviours you would like to see more of, and less of, and be prepared to give reasons for both. Sales targets, customer service, housekeeping and teamwork are common areas for review.

For example:

More of	Less of
Sharing your customer service skills with others. (How do you do it?)	Complaints about sharing the duties for housekeeping.
Up-to-the-minute product knowledge on new items.	Making long personal calls on the telephone during your shift.

2. Help the Staff Member Get His or Her Thoughts Together

Let your staff member know that you want to have a conversation about his or her performance and make an appointment for the meeting. Be sure to explain that the purpose is to:

- O acknowledge strengths
- O discuss how he or she has contributed to the store
- O consider areas for growth and development
- O generally look at the picture for the last six months or so
- O discuss plans for the next season(s).

Be aware that even this non-threatening approach can create some stress for your staff. One store manager discovered that one of his top performers took a tranquillizer before the performance review meeting. The manager vowed to pay more attention to the unconscious ways he raised the stress of his staff. Here is a small memo he gives to staff now.

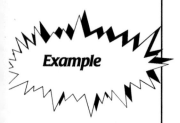

Our Review

Purposes of our conversation:

- O *See the big picture of your skills and strengths*
- O *Celebrate your achievements*
- O *Identify any areas for improvement and set goals*
- O *Have a chance to think together about your work here.*

Please think about: sales, customer service, your non-selling duties, your achievements and where you think you might need to improve. Please think about the ways we can support your success and what you need from me to be even more successful in the future.

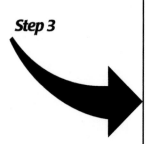

3. Schedule Some Uninterrupted Time

Be sure you have set aside time that will allow you to conduct the review privately, without being interrupted. Be prepared to take a half hour to an hour. Don't expect to deal with it thoroughly in 10 – 15 minutes. You won't get the results you want.

If uninterrupted time is almost an impossibility in your store, consider taking the person out to lunch or have the meeting in some quiet place. Some retailers establish a relationship with a restaurant owner or manager and arrange to have coffee and their conversation at a back table when the restaurant is least busy.

4. Set a Positive Tone

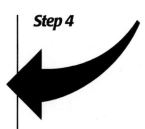

Step 4

The goal is to offer support and encouragement through an open and honest approach. This tone should be set at the very beginning. If the review process is new for the staff member, he or she may be nervous about it. This is another reason to begin on a positive note.

Manager: *Tomas, in the next half hour, I hope we can talk frankly about your contribution last season. I have appreciated your efforts and your positive attitude. Let's talk about what worked well, what didn't work so well and what we have learned that can help you to be even more successful in the coming months. We should consider any changes you could make and anything I can do to support you. Let's begin by reviewing some of your accomplishments.*

5. Start with Something Positive

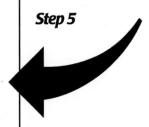

Step 5

We all like to hear good news and praise. Make sure you begin on a positive note. Talk about what you appreciate – sales volume, teamwork, growth you have seen, or special achievements. Ask what the staff person sees as a personal strength, an achievement, growth, etc. Make this a conversation – not a speech.

Compliment the staff member on specific strengths or positive contributions they have made recently. It is more effective and practical to discuss specific behaviour than to discuss attitude because it is easier to observe, describe and change behaviour.

See also Chapter 5

Avoid "Attitude" – Don't Say	Discuss Behaviour – Do Say
You have a wonderful attitude toward the customers!	*You really listen to your customers and take time to find out what they really want. That makes such a difference!*
You have a bad attitude toward the other people on the floor.	*Yesterday you didn't help other staff members when they were busy and you didn't have a customer.*

Step 6

Step 7

opportunities for performance improvement, and new or expanded areas of responsibility

6. Involve the Staff Member

The review process will not be successful if it is a one-way conversation. This is not a report about how you feel about the staff member. It should be an open discussion between two people both concerned with future success – a partnership. Asking questions and really listening to your staff member's thoughts and opinions will encourage him or her to take an active role in the conversation. If you are not sure what your staff thinks about a topic, ask questions before giving your opinion or reaction. If you see things differently, accept these differences. Explore why you hold different views, and how you can move forward.

Manager:	*You moved to the home entertainment department three months ago. How has that changed your job?*
Sam:	*It was really tough at first. There was so much to learn. But now I like it. The equipment is fun to sell. I've always been interested in it, even though I didn't know much about it.*
Manager:	*Has it been difficult to learn the technical side of things?*
Sam:	*Well I must admit I had no idea there were so many differences among the televisions and VCRs that we sell. But now I'm getting the hang of it – and the other people in the department have been really good.*
Manager:	*Are there any areas where you feel you need to increase your own product knowledge?*
Sam:	*Yes! I'd like to know about video cameras and the new fuzzy logic feature.*

7. Focus on Positive Change

Talk about opportunities for performance improvement, and when appropriate, new or expanded areas of responsibility.

Be specific about the changes you require and be sure to give the reason for the change. Whenever possible, involve the staff member in the decision about how long it will take to make the change and how it will happen. Talk about areas for improvement in a positive, supportive way. Let the staff member know that you realize that change is something we all have to deal with and that it's not always easy or fast.

Manager:	*I think we've agreed that housekeeping is not one of your favourite activities. Like many of us, if given a choice, you'd rather spend time with a customer. But we do need to make sure the housekeeping side of the job gets done every day. As a member of the sales team, it is important that you do your part or others will be resentful. Does that make sense to you? What would make it easier for you to get the vacuuming done and do a thorough job?*

Manager: *I think we have agreed that you are doing an excellent job in some areas and very acceptable work in these other areas. It's time to offer you some opportunities for growth. I want to include you in more of the buying decisions and help you learn about all the considerations that go into this part of the business. How would you like that?*

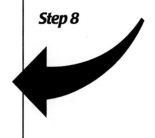

Step 8

8. Check for Obstacles to High Performance

What, if anything, might get in the way of continued high performance? What might be obstacles or roadblocks to making desired changes? Be sure to provide an encouraging and supportive tone that will draw out the employee. Silence can be very effective here, if it is paired with a look of interest and an encouraging nod or gesture.

See probing techniques on page 106

Manager: *Thinking about your agreement to do your share of restocking the goods, can you think of any roadblocks that will get in the way of your following through?*

Sid: *Well, I get pretty busy sometimes. I might forget to do it.*

Manager: *I know it's hard to remember everything. What could you do to help yourself remember?*

Sid: *Maybe I could try to do it at the same time every day – maybe just before I go to lunch. That way I wouldn't be so likely to forget. I never forget lunch!*

Manager: *(Laughing) That's true! And that would be a good time to do it; you are already moving out of your sales role to leave for lunch, so it could be a transition. Be prepared to rotate this time with the other staff who prefer it also.*

Sid: *That sounds okay. I'll tell the others. Then they'll keep me honest as well.*

It is often in these conversations that the manager can learn about systems problems, that is, store systems or rules that get in the way. If obstacles do surface, take them seriously and work with staff input to remove them or reduce their impact on the situation. Develop a clear and specific plan for dealing with the problem.

How can you remove the obstacles to great performance?

Who Decides What a Staff Member Should Do Differently?

If you find that you are telling a person over and over again to do something and they don't do it, one of several things may be happening: they don't believe that what you are asking them to do is important or that they will be recognized or rewarded for doing it; they don't understand what you are asking for; they don't have the skills; the store systems are blocking them. If you ask them to take more initiative, don't be surprised when they do not, if you are requiring them to get your signature for every refund, every special sale, and other areas of decision-making that they could handle. If you expect everyone to be a team player, tell them. Then show you mean it by judging their performance in terms of their contribution to the team.

If you want the staff member to really be committed to making changes, you need to involve them fully in the decision to change. As the manager, you provide input and suggestions.

The staff person will also have suggestions to make. Ultimately, the decision about whether to change or not rests with the staff person. The decision will depend on the person's willingness to change and the value or reasons that person associates with the change. What you can do as manager is clarify the consequences for both the store and the staff member of the person's current behaviour and the proposed changes.

9. Summarize the Discussion

As the review comes to an end, summarize the discussion including strengths, any areas requiring change, and any new opportunities. Discuss goals you have set together. Be sure to note any actions that have been agreed to, and how long it will take to make them happen. Be clear about who is responsible for what, and how this review will be followed up.

Manager: *We've certainly agreed that you are making an excellent contribution around here. The two areas that need attention are restocking and technical knowledge of the new video equipment. You agreed to give the merchandising responsibilities a higher priority by doing them thoroughly every day. I'll talk to our suppliers and arrange for you to attend the next technical seminar they offer on the video cameras. I think you'll really enjoy that.*

Manager: *We've reviewed the contribution you are making to the team. Your colleagues obviously rely on your technical expertise and your willingness to help them. You seemed pleased with my request to involve you more formally in orienting new staff. You have agreed to review how we do it, and develop a plan for improving it. I'll be pleased to have you work with me to bring the seasonal staff on board in a more effective way.*

Step 9

strengths, any areas requiring change, and any new opportunities

10. End on a Positive Note

There are many ways to end on a positive note. Here are a few of them:

- ○ Thank the person for their contribution during the past season.

- ○ Encourage them to keep learning and developing their skills.

- ○ Assure them that you are prepared to offer continued support.

- ○ Encourage them to ask for help or assistance, as needed.

- ○ Invite them to make suggestions about how the store can be improved.

- ○ Show your own enthusiasm for their plan of action and the positive changes planned.

- ○ Express your confidence in their ability to continue to make a positive contribution.

Finally, no matter what else you say, THANK THEM for their time, their ideas and for being an active part of the review.

Express your confidence in their ability to continue to make a positive contribution

ADDITIONAL GUIDELINES FOR REVIEW DISCUSSIONS WITH STAFF

Here are several guidelines that should be reflected in every stage of the review process:

- ○ **No surprises!** You don't like surprises; neither does your staff. Don't spring a new complaint or concern that has not been discussed before on a staff member during the review. This process should look at the "big picture" by summarizing things that are already known to both of you.

- ○ **Be positive!** Positive expectations are more likely to lead to positive results. Expect a lot from people and you are likely to get it. Expect very little and that's what you will get. Assume the person wants to do well and make a positive contribution.

- ○ **Be fair.** Treat people in a fair, honest and open manner. Don't play favourites. Don't enforce the rules with one person and be lax with another. That doesn't mean that your expectations have to be the same for everyone or that everyone must be treated in exactly the same way. See the chapter on Assigning Work for more on this topic.

- ○ **Be honest with staff.** Sometimes it is difficult to be honest when you anticipate that you may upset the other person. It is better for them to know how you really feel and what you expect than not to know. At least if they know, they can choose to respond and make positive changes.

○ **Set measurable standards.** Be prepared to explain how you arrived at your expectations for store performance and staff performance, and what you use as indicators of progress and success. There is an old saying: "What gets measured gets done." Don't limit your measured results to sales. Find ways to measure other aspects of performance that you think are important. What do you watch and listen for to monitor a "positive attitude toward customer service?" Describe these behaviours instead of using vague terms like "attitude."

○ **Write down your own commitments to follow up.** Don't forget to keep your part of the bargain. If you agreed to do something, write it down in your daily planner and make sure you do it. Don't let the staff member down by not doing your part to support change.

REVIEWING YOUR PERFORMANCE

The more you invite staff to give you feedback on your performance, the more:

○ you will learn about your strengths and areas for growth

○ you will be able to tailor what you do to their needs

○ you will identify systems problems that limit success

○ open they will become to receiving your feedback.

Think about how you want to ask your staff for information on your work with them. The self-assessment forms that appear in every chapter of this book can be used by staff to give you feedback. You can also ask open-ended questions like:

○ What am I doing that helps you?

○ What do you wish I would start to do or do more of?

○ What do you wish I would stop doing or do less of?

Answers to these questions can be a rich resource for you and your business if you stay open to the ideas of your staff. Avoid thinking in "right" or "wrong" terms. Take the attitude of: "What can I learn?"

Whether you think you can or you think you can't – you will be right

ACTION PLANNING

Perhaps the ideas in this chapter have stimulated your thinking and you have identified some ideas you want to remember. The discipline of writing these ideas in the space below will serve you in two ways. First, jotting them down will help you remember them. Second, finding the ideas again will be easy if they are summarized, with references to the pages in this chapter, on one page.

Page	Ideas I Want To Apply	Other Notes to Yourself
____	_____	_____
____	_____	_____
____	_____	_____
____	_____	_____
____	_____	_____
____	_____	_____
____	_____	_____
____	_____	_____
____	_____	_____
____	_____	_____
____	_____	_____
____	_____	_____
____	_____	_____
____	_____	_____

SAMPLE PERFORMANCE REVIEW FORMS

Here are several forms to consider. Remember that the choice of a form is not nearly as important as the discussion you have with your staff members. The form can provide you with a guide to keep the discussion on track.

Performance Review For:	Covers the Period From _____ To _____			
Performance Area	Achievement Level			Notes and Goals
	Under Expectations	Meets Expectations	Above Expectations	
Customer Relations				
Asking Questions				
Demonstrating Features and Benefits				
Responding to Objections				
Handling Add-ons				
Closing				
Encouraging Repeat Business				
Handling Problems				
Telephone Contact				
Sales				
Teamwork				
Housekeeping				
Merchandising				
Punctuality and Presence				
Interest in Learning				
Creativity				

RATING SCALES

As you can see, the previous form used a rating scale. Here are some other examples of rating scales:

Needs Improvement	Acceptable	Excellent
Below Average	Average	Above Average
Does Not Meet Expectations	Meets Expectations	Exceeds Expectations

OPEN QUESTIONS

Other forms, like the next two samples, simply list key areas and leave space for comments.

Performance Review for _____ (Covers Period from _____ to _____)
Sales Performance (Sales relative to targets, sales relative to store average):
Customer Service Performance (Letters, comments, etc.):
Housekeeping (Cleanliness):
Merchandising (Display maintenance):
Attendance and Punctuality:
Willingness to Pitch In:
Special Qualities:
Goals and Wishes:

FILL IN THE BLANKS

Here is a fairly simple form that covers many of the key issues in a review. It invites staff input and provides questions for them to think about before you meet. Note that it invites discussion of your role in helping staff achieve success.

1. During the season, how did you perform/contribute to sales?

   (a) sales/hour _____

   (b) units/sale _____

   (c) accessories _____

2. During the season, how did you perform/contribute in the non-selling areas?

   _____

   _____

3. During the season, how did you contribute to building repeat business for the store?

   _____

   _____

4. During the season, what are you most proud of? _____

   _____

5. During the season, what did you learn? _____

   _____

6. What do you want to work at, improve or learn next season? _____

   _____

7. What new things have you tried? What worked for you? _____

   _____

8. What plans or resources will you need to help you achieve this? _____

   _____

9. How can I help you? _____

   _____

"BOTTOM LINE" SUMMARY

This approach focuses quickly on results!

Review for _____ Covers Period from _____ to _____

1. Your sales results against goal. _____

   _____

   _____

2. Your sales results against store average. _____

   _____

   _____

3. Non-selling duties you performed. _____

   _____

   _____

4. Things that I liked. _____

   _____

   _____

5. Things that I didn't like. _____

   _____

   _____

6. Plans for next season. _____

   _____

   _____

7. Overall Rating: ____ Exceeded Expectations/Standards

                       ____ Met Expectations/Standards

                       ____ Did Not Meet Expectations/Standards

---

Turning Performance Problems Into Productivity

This chapter will:

✓ identify possible causes of performance problems

✓ discuss your role in resolving performance problems

✓ provide a model for assessing what's going wrong, and alternative solutions

✓ offer strategies for handling staff's personal problems

✓ give practical advice on how to handle tough conversations

✓ suggest ways to respond to challenging behaviours

WHY PERFORMANCE PROBLEMS?

There are many reasons why staff members might have performance problems. Sometimes their knowledge, skills and experience don't match the needs of the job. Other times, the reasons relate more to their willingness and sense of confidence. Between the two extremes of ignoring poor performance and firing the person, there are many things you can do to get the staff member back "on track."

Start by assessing the situation. Think of a situation in which you have had a performance problem with a staff member. Jot down a few notes and refer to them as you go through this chapter.

I am thinking of _____ whose performance in the following areas has been unacceptable:

○

○

○

○

○

○

○

Keeping this person's performance in mind, you may find it interesting to do the situation analysis on the next page.

A SITUATION ANALYSIS

*Read each item on the left below and check off
the box that best reflects your assessment*

Rate the following in terms of how well they were done:	did this well	did this ok	needed more attention	not relevant
1. How would you rate the interviewing for the job?				
2. Were the expectations for this job well defined?				
3. Was the person brought on board effectively?				
4. Was this person informed that he or she would be evaluated on the performance of their job, and how this would be done?				
5. Are his or her talents and skills being used appropriately?				
6. Has this person been receiving the support and encouragement he or she needed to be successful?				
7. Has this person been treated with respect? Listened to?				
8. Did this person get enough coaching and training?				
9. When the job was not done properly, was this person told about it?				
10. Are expectations clear? Realistic?				
11. Was the person given an opportunity to improve?				
12. Were the consequences of poor performance clearly outlined?				
TOTAL CHECK MARKS				
Multiply by	multiply by 3	multiply by 2	multiply by 1	multiply by 0
TOTAL SCORE				
GRAND TOTAL – add columns 1 + 2 + 3				

Interpretation:

0 – 12   There has been virtually no support for good performance.

13 – 24   There is a long way to go to correct poor performance.

25 – 36   There is support for staff to succeed.

SITUATION ANALYSIS

The situation analysis on the previous page identifies the factors that support high performance. When you assess the person's performance and find it less than acceptable, you must ask what role the store played in making that happen, and what role you played.

Look for the problems in your policies and practices ... before you pin them on your people

First, discovering the role the store played means examining store policies and systems. Are they supporting sales and the work of the staff? For example, is the markdown system so time-consuming that staff have to fit sales and service around it?

Second, is it your role to ensure that the store is successful? Is it your role to support the staff who can make or break the store? How has your performance been? Keeping in mind the situation you identified at the beginning of this chapter, ask yourself **in relation to each item** on the assessment:

○ Should I have done the work myself to get a rating of "doing this well"?

○ Should I have assigned it to others? Should I have checked up on what was done?

○ What has to be done to make sure that, **in the future,** we can rate every item "did this well"?

Having assessed what has happened, the path to avoiding performance problems in the future is clear. It may take a while to set yourself up to be able to check the "did this very well" category for every item, and it will be worth it in the long run. And other retailers have done it!

In the short term, what do you do with this staff person? Take one more look at yourself to see how you are part of the problem and part of the solution.

Some managers think performance problems happen because staff:

○ can't figure out how to do any better

○ want to get by with as little effort as possible

○ don't really care

○ don't understand what is expected of them

○ were not the right ones for the job

○ have not been groomed to succeed.

Why do you think performance problems happen? Your beliefs are central to what happens in your store. Your beliefs can create self-fulfilling prophecies.

WHAT IS A SELF-FULFILLING PROPHECY?

"Seeing is believing." You often hear this phrase even though research studies have shown that reality is the exact opposite! We tend to see what we believe we will see, and we look for information to confirm our beliefs and actions.

Advertisers know this. Who is most likely to read an ad or article for a particular item like a new car? The person who has just purchased it and the person who has already made up their mind to buy one! Not what you would imagine. The readers aren't searching for new information. They are confirming what they already believe.

You will see it when you believe it.

Wayne Dyer

When people are not performing to expectation, do you tend to be on the look-out for the mistakes? Are you labelling them "poor performers"? Could you be missing their successes?

An important research study from Harvard tells us just how powerful our beliefs are.

> At the beginning of the school year, one group of teachers (call them "A" teachers) were told that their students were very smart – high achievers. The others (call them "B" teachers) were told that the students in their class were not smart – low achievers.

> The children were assigned to the classes in the following way: the "smart" children were sent to the "B" teachers and the "not smart" children to the "A" teachers. Guess whose grades rose? Guess whose grades fell? Right, the "smart" children's grades fell under the condition of having teachers who believed they did not have ability. The reverse happened for the children who were labelled low achievers. They did really well under the teachers who had been led to believe that they were smart.

So, what are your beliefs about the person whose performance is not what it needs to be? Do you think this person can do the job? Are you communicating your beliefs and affecting how the person is performing?

CONSIDER TWO QUESTIONS. DO YOU THINK THIS PERSON:

1. **can develop** into a good performer in your store? If so,

   ○ prepare yourself for the type of challenging conversation described later in this chapter

   ○ ensure you can make the time, or your staff can make the time, to coach and support change.

2. **will not** become a good performer in your store? If so,

   ○ prepare yourself for a challenging conversation

   ○ ensure you understand what you need to do to respect the provincial and federal regulations (labour code) in case of dismissal. If you are in a setting where there is a collective agreement, ensure you respect the stages in the process.

If you are not sure what might be required for the person to become a good performer, consider what it takes for a person to change, and the support needed.

HOW DO PEOPLE CHANGE THEIR BEHAVIOUR?

Think of one of the toughest challenges you face in bringing about change in the behaviour of your staff. Does it relate to housekeeping duties, remembering to thank customers for their business, or remembering how to close the sale? In all these cases, the staff member may have to go through all six stages of a change process:

1. **Awareness**

   Staff have to be aware of or see the need to do something differently. Some people only know one way of making a sale or putting out the garbage. They need to learn about alternatives.

2. **Understanding**

   They need to understand the reasons for a change. They need to have reasons that make sense **for them.** "My boss thinks it will work" doesn't have lasting motivational impact.

3. **Decision**

   They need to "buy in" – believe in the value of the change and be willing to act on it. Instead of doing it because they were told to, they need to do it because they want to. People ask themselves: "Do I think this is worth doing?" and "Do I think I will be capable of doing it?"

4. **Trial Action**

   They need to try it out, to test it and assess it for themselves. Some people just won't accept something until they can experience for themselves that it works.

5. **Practice**

   They need to practise the behaviour over and over **with** encouragement, reinforcement and feedback. You need to be willing to accept the mistakes that are likely to happen as people practise. You need to ensure that time is made available for practice and that you support the staff learning and the new behaviour. Some research indicates that it can take up to 21 days for a new behaviour to become a habit. Be patient. Change takes time. The practice will lead to new habits.

6. **New Habits**

   The changed behaviour will become habit.

If you think you can – or if you think you can't – you will be right.

Anonymous

DEVELOPING HIGH PERFORMING STAFF

If you are getting resistance from your staff, perhaps they are not ready. If, at any step in the change process, a staff person gets stuck, they will not be able to move forward and complete the change successfully.

On page 210 you identified a situation. Think about it in relation to the six steps. Is the person ready and willing to make a change? Is the person stuck somewhere along the way? What could you do to help them get unstuck and move forward?

At stages 1 and 2 (gaining awareness and understanding), people need information. It's helpful to hear options, and consider the pros and cons of doing or not doing something.

At stage 3 (decision-making), it is important to have information about the value of the change, the consequences of not changing, the coaching or support there will be for trying out new behaviour, the tolerance for mistakes, and how to avoid any embarrassment that might be associated with deciding to change.

At stages 4 and 5 (trial action and practice), people need encouragement and feedback.

TWO KINDS OF ISSUES – AND HOW TO ADDRESS THEM

There are two basic reasons why someone might have trouble following through on their agreed upon responsibilities.

1. Capability Issues

The staff members may not know what to do or how to do it. These are issues of **expectations** and **preparedness.**

2. Willingness Issues

The staff members may not be **motivated** to behave the way you want them to or they may lack the **self-confidence** to try.

In the next section, each type of problem is described with strategies for addressing it. While you read it, it will be helpful to keep the same person you had in mind at the beginning of this chapter, or someone else who is not performing well.

About practising:
You always pass failure on your way to success.

Mickey Rooney

See also Chapter 10

1. Improving Capability

For Someone Who Does Not Know What Is Expected (Expectations Problems):

○ **Clarify what is expected (who, what, when, where, why, how?).**

Take the time needed to reorient the person. They may have forgotten some things or never understood what was required. Clear expectations and standards are essential. Discuss the right and wrong ways to do the job and the reasons for your preferred way of doing things.

○ **Observe the person on the job.**

If you really don't know why the person is performing poorly, it may help to watch them do the job. You may pick up on errors you never expected or discussed. This will give you an excellent basis for further discussion, reorientation or training.

For Someone Who Doesn't Know How (Preparedness Problems):

○ **Model ("Show and Tell").**

Show the person how to do the job, task or activity. Demonstrate it yourself or link the staff member with someone else who already has the knowledge and skills.

○ **Create opportunities for practice.**

Give the person a chance to improve through supervised practice. Role play situations and create trial practice opportunities. Make sure that this is done in an environment where he or she can get feedback and encouragement and where making a few mistakes will not create serious problems.

○ **Coach – provide clear information on the likely effects of various approaches.**

Coach on the right and wrong way to do the job. Let the person know the type of problems that can occur if they proceed in an inappropriate way. Explain the positive things that will happen when the approaches you recommend are used.

○ **Provide technical training.**

Send the person to courses, seminars, workshops or training sessions. Many associations offer excellent courses in selling skills, customer service, product knowledge. Find out what your Association offers.

2. Improving Willingness

There are two basic obstacles that will interfere with the staff member's willingness. They are: **lack of self-confidence** (they are afraid they will make mistakes or fail) and **lack of motivation** (they don't want to do the job because they don't enjoy it or value it).

For Confidence Problems:

○ **Create achievable steps.**

Simplify the assignment by breaking big or complex tasks into smaller "chunks." This can make the work less threatening as well as provide more opportunities for the staff member to get assistance and advice. As a result, the staff member will probably be less reluctant to take on the work because the personal risk will be lower.

Situational management Style 1 or Style 2 – see Chapter 10

○ **Reinforce the right way to do the job through clear, positive feedback.**

Sometimes we just don't provide enough feedback on what is working and what is not. The staff member feels uncertain or confused about what is expected and what is acceptable.

○ **Encourage experimentation.**

Sometimes it's not possible for you to explain exactly how a job should be done. Give staff a clear idea of the desirable outcomes and then allow them the freedom to accomplish the task in their own way. Let them know that their own experimentation is valued and perfection is not expected.

Stand beside, not over

○ **Provide reassurance and support for attempts at improvement.**

Let the staff member know that you appreciate their attempts to improve. Create an atmosphere in which mistakes are welcomed, because more can be learned by trying new methods and making mistakes than from sticking to past methods that are safe but ineffective.

For Lack of Motivation:

○ **Initiate supportive, non-judgemental conversation.**

Sometimes the best strategy involves more listening and less talking. Meet with the person and ask why their performance has changed. What is happening for that person? There may be some factors at work here that you know nothing about. Once they are in the open, you will be able to deal with them.

○ **Provide recognition and appreciation.**

People like to be appreciated. If the staff person's efforts have not been recognized or valued in the past, it may be difficult for them to get excited about putting forth the same or greater effort on a consistent basis. Providing a lot of sincere appreciation can make staff feel much more positive about the work.

○ **Clarify the consequences for different levels of performance.**

Sometimes, you do have to remind an unmotivated staff member that there is a relationship between their behaviour and the way they are treated as a staff member. Negative consequences (e.g. fewer hours) should be balanced with positive consequences (e.g. recognition, bonuses).

Before reading on, you might benefit from applying the ideas thus far. You might want to return to the performance problem you identified on the first page of this chapter or identify a new one. What can you do to encourage an improvement in the skills or willingness of the staff member?

Person: _____

In what way is performance poor?:
(e.g. Does not use suggestion selling, functions more like an order-taker.) _____

_____

_____

Underlying Problems: **Capability:** ❏ Expectations ❏ Preparedness
(Knowledge, Skills)

Willingness: ❏ Self-confidence ❏ Motivation

Strategies: *(e.g. **Salesperson to:** Find mix and match item for every sweater. Add accessories. If stuck, ask the manager or other staff for help. Demonstrate in role plays with manager and staff how the items go together. Observe other staff selling multiples. **Manager to:** Encourage and provide feedback. Set target date for first multiple sale)*

_____

_____

_____

_____

_____

_____

_____

_____

_____

CHALLENGING CONVERSATIONS

Although it is not always easy to talk with someone about poor performance, it is possible to make the conversation supportive, respectful and meaningful. The steps below are similar to the steps in the performance review conversation, as outlined in Chapter 12.

1. Prepare Yourself.

Step 1

Think about the things you want to talk about:

○ What have been the performance issues (behaviour, frequency, seriousness)?

○ What has the impact of these behaviours been on the store, the staff, you and the person you are talking with?

○ What discussions have already taken place regarding these behaviours (recall the dates, times and agreements)?

○ What do you appreciate about this person?

○ What strengths and potential do you see in this person?

○ What do you want to have happen?

○ What are you willing to do to make this happen?

○ What do you need to do to make sure that you listen, clarify, and acknowledge feelings?

2. Lay the Foundation for a Candid, Respectful Conversation.

Step 2

Start off by describing your hopes for the conversation. Lay the foundation for respect, mutual support and, if possible, a long-term appreciation for each other. No matter how you feel about this person, remember that many factors contributed to their performance. Even if the conversation ends up in a termination or resignation, you can still give the person your respect and appreciation for whatever they have done for you.

See Chapter 5 on giving feedback

Manager: *It's my hope that when this conversation is over, we will both feel that we have had a candid and respectful discussion about your future. I am not sure where this conversation will lead. I am sure that I want to talk about two things: what I appreciate about the work you have done, and what has to happen to improve your performance. I also want to hear your thoughts and ideas. Let me start by summarizing the situation.*

3. Provide Feedback.

Step 3

What has been happening? What has been the impact? Be specific.

4. Ask for Staff Person's View and Hopes.

An open-ended question such as, "What do you think we should do now?" or "How can we fix this problem?" can be very helpful. You will want to:

- ○ listen very carefully
- ○ ask questions to clarify
- ○ summarize what you have heard
- ○ acknowledge feelings.

This will give you an idea of what the person is expecting and what the person is prepared to do.

Your desired outcome is to solve the problem and keep the relationship as positive as possible. Stay open to learning from what the person says about the work, the store, the staff, even about you. If the questions you ask lead to expression of upset feelings, take time to hear both the head and heart of the other person. You do not have to give up your standards by doing so.

See also Chapters 3 and 4 on listening and acknowledging feelings

5. Describe What You are Prepared to Do and What You Want.

Now it's time to explain your point of view. Indicate the areas where the two of you are in agreement about what needs to happen. Make yourself clear about what you expect or need for an acceptable solution to the problem.

6. Try to Solve the Problem.

Are there solutions that will work for both of you? Explore alternatives. Look for points of agreement. If none can be found, at least you and the staff person know that both of you have tried.

7. Come to a Decision About the Next Steps.

If it doesn't look like there will be change, ask for a resignation or arrange for the person to leave. Make sure your actions comply with provincial regulations, the federal Employment Standards Act, and the policies of your organization. In a setting where there is a union, respect the collective agreement.

Remember your role in C.P.R

If the staff person is willing to change, offer the help you can provide. Ask what the person will commit to and develop a plan of action. Include agreements about what will happen by what date, and what the consequences will be if the changes do not occur. You may want to follow up with a written summary of the conversation and the next steps. If so, advise the person and follow up later. There is a sample performance improvement agreement on page 226.

8. Express Appreciation.

Thank the person for taking the time to deal with this difficult matter. If you have come to a performance agreement, express confidence in the person's ability to make the agreed-to changes.

HINTS FOR HEADING OFF UNNECESSARY HEAT

No Surprises

If you have been doing your job as store manager, there should be no surprises for the staff member. Everything discussed should already be known by both parties. During the conversation about performance, examine the patterns or issues rather than focus on individual incidents.

Good Record-keeping and Documentation

In the earlier chapters on effective communication, the high potential for misunderstandings was explained. As time passes after a stressful conversation, the details of what was said can be forgotten or altered. It is important to confirm major issues or concerns in writing. A written record, that both parties review, is especially important in situations that may lead to grievances or terminations.

Have Positive Expectations

Expect positive, open communication and a commitment to a positive contribution to the workplace. You will be much more likely to get this if you expect it.

Be Sensitive to the Person's Sense of Self-Worth

Don't be heavy-handed. Use only what is required for the problem to be solved in a positive, productive way. Don't over-kill.

Be Ready for Excuses or Confrontation

Consistently demonstrate to staff members that excuses, challenges, and confrontation will not be effective in your conversations about performance and standards (or anywhere else in the working relationship).

SOME CHALLENGING SCENARIOS

Managers often ask what to do when the staff member:

1. gets really upset

2. gives excuses and tries to deflect attention from the issue

3. has a personal problem.

1. How Do You Respond to Someone Who is Really Upset?

What if, despite all the planning and preventive measures described above, the person gets very upset? Clearly, the conversation will not be able to progress if there is a lot of emotional tension. Here are some ways to reduce the tension:

Use Good Listening Techniques to Lower Tension

If you are faced with someone who is upset, you will need to find a way to help them calm down before you can discuss an action plan with them. Take the time to really listen to their concern. Ask open-ended questions and be prepared to listen until they finish. Don't interrupt or try to "shortcut" their discussion. If they don't get a chance to express their feelings, they won't be able to approach any problem-solving in an effective way.

Acknowledge Their Feelings

This can be a simple statement, such as: "I can see that you are really upset," or "This seems to have been a very frustrating situation for you." Don't deny their feelings with comments such as "Don't feel bad," or "You shouldn't be upset." This will make matters worse. Let them know that you are aware that they feel very strongly about this and that you understand why they might feel upset.

Good decisions cannot be made until strong emotions have subsided. If you proceed with problem-solving, it probably won't be effective.

2. How Do You Deal With Excuses or "Deflections"

When people are confronted with what they think is criticism, their tension will start to rise. They might try to "deflect" the issue by switching to another topic. This would take the pressure off and give more control of the situation. Deflections can take many forms. They include excuses, blame, counter-accusations, immediate agreement, etc. Here are some typical responses that might be made to a concern about being late:

- ○ *I'm not the only person that comes late!*

- ○ *What about all the extra time I put in?*

- ○ *It's not my fault, I have an old car.*

- ○ *It's not easy getting kids to the babysitter before work, you know.*

Each of these is an attempt to both express a perception and remove the pressure for a change in performance. Don't let go of the need to ensure standards are met. Do follow up on off-hand comments that suggest favouritism or unfairness. For example:

- ○ *Is it your perception that it's OK for others to come in late and that it's not OK for you? I want to make sure I'm being fair so we need to discuss this. What specifically are you referring to?*

Then, remember to return to this person's performance! Another effective approach is to acknowledge the statement made to deflect you and then return to the real issue. The following are some responses to the examples of deflections shown on the previous page. They follow a format of "When you..., I feel..., because...."

○ *I realize that other people are late for work too. But right now we are talking about you. When you're late for work, the staff feel resentful because they have to cover for you.*

○ *You certainly do put in a lot of extra time, and it's appreciated. But when you come late, I feel angry because I do not want to spend my time wondering when you will arrive so that I can do my work instead of covering for you.*

Acknowledge that you heard the other person but make it clear that you are not going to get side-tracked into irrelevant issues or unreasonable excuses. Of course, if the conversation brings up a valid reason that you were unaware of, this new concern would have to be recognized and addressed in a sensitive manner.

Don't push too hard to be right on small, insignificant points. Sometimes it's worth letting go on a small technical matter in order to focus on the big issues. Don't waste time arguing over an actual sales figure when you really want to discuss why sales weren't achieved. You have the right to define standards and expect performance.

3. When Personal Problems Affect Work Performance

When personal problems (such as relationships or financial problems, substance abuse, etc.) are affecting a staff member, you must maintain a careful balance between providing assistance for the staff member and protecting the store. Here are some suggestions for fulfilling both your responsibilities in a fair and reasonable way:

Focus on the performance

Collect the Necessary Data

○ Establish the levels of work performance you expect and write them down. Decide how much of a decline in job performance you will tolerate before you take action.

○ Record all absenteeism, poor job performance, etc. Include examples of specific behaviour.

○ Be consistent in your expectations. Don't play favourites.

○ Don't try to diagnose the problem or determine what personal problems may exist. Deal only with declining job performance.

Discuss the Problem with the Staff Member

○ Approach the staff member on the basis of declining work performance.

○ Be firm and honest. The staff member will respect you for it.

○ Be ready to cope with the staff member's resistance, defensiveness and even hostility.

○ Don't accept excuses for failure. There is no legitimate excuse for prolonged, impaired job performance.

○ Avoid making moral judgements. It is better to tell the staff members what you expect than to tell them what they should or shouldn't do.

Agree on a Plan of Action

○ Be specific about the behaviour as it relates to performance. Aspects of the plan, such as time lines and expected outcomes, must be clear and attainable.

○ Remember that it is the staff member's responsibility to improve job performance by seeking help.

○ Your Retail Association may have a list of resources available in your community and further information on how to handle a variety of personal problems.

C.P.R.

Monitor Progress

○ Ensure that a plan is set up so that both you and the staff member will know if progress is made. Evaluate the staff member's progress together.

○ If, after some improvement, a staff member begins to slip in job performance again, review and discuss the action plan.

○ When performance improves, praise the staff member. Recognition of good work will reinforce the desirable job performance.

ACTION PLANNING

What ideas do you want to remember	Page #	When and How Do You Want to Implement Them	Who Can Help You?	By When?

PERFORMANCE IMPROVEMENT AGREEMENT

This is a record of:
- ○ first conversation about these issues
- ○ second conversation about these issues
- ○ third conversation about these issues

Conversation between: _____ and _____

Held on: _____

This notice identifies:

○ attendance issues   ○ productivity issues   ○ customer service issues

○ team relations issues   ○ violations of company policy

○ other _____

Comments re Events and Behaviours:

Agreed to Next Steps:

Signed by _____ Date: _____

Signed by _____ Date: _____

Staff Motivation

This chapter will:

✓ provide insights on motivation from successful retailers

✓ report research on what makes employees want to stay and work

✓ apply the research to your staff and your store

✓ illustrate how different motivations compete

✓ offer one explanation of the process of changing emotions

✓ describe how to match the motivational offerings in a job with staff needs

✓ describe your role in motivating yourself and your staff

MOTIVATION

Use the following rating scale to indicate how frequently you do the following:

1 point = rarely
2 points = sometimes
3 points = very often

_____ 1. I provide opportunities for my staff to be creative and show initiative.

_____ 2. I ask my staff to share in the planning and decision-making for the store.

_____ 3. I encourage my staff to grow in knowledge, skills and experience.

_____ 4. I develop an atmosphere of trust and mutual respect.

_____ 5. I support a team approach in the store.

_____ 6. I encourage everyone to contribute to the success of the store.

_____ 7. I help my staff develop their own career potential.

_____ 8. I provide each staff person opportunities for a sense of personal accomplishment and success in the work they do.

_____ 9. I make sure store goals and objectives are shared with staff.

_____ 10. I explain my expectations as clearly as possible.

_____ 11. I show my appreciation for staff's contributions.

_____ 12. I provide clear and regular feedback on the quality of work so staff know where they stand.

_____ 13. I ask staff for ideas and suggestions and consider their opinions carefully.

_____ 14. I look for ways to celebrate individual and group achievements.

_____ 15. I provide staff with varied and interesting work assignments.

_____ 16. I look for ways to give staff more of the kinds of work they enjoy.

_____ 17. I show my staff I have confidence in their abilities.

_____ 18. I encourage staff members to support each other.

_____ 19. I support an environment where we enjoy our work and have fun.

_____ 20. I care about my staff and I let them know it!

_____ **TOTAL SCORE**

Interpretation:

1 – 20   You may be a road-block to high performing staff.

21 – 40   You are well on your way to having a motivated team.

41 – 60   You have a highly motivated.

MOTIVATION FROM THE RETAILERS' POINT OF VIEW

Retail is full of highly motivated people. People who work hard and love the action of it all. People who work long hours and love the customers. People who love the product. People who like to work alone. People who thrive on teamwork. People who are energized by challenge and change.

Not everyone would entirely agree with the previous paragraph. Some store owners and managers experience staff who try to get by with as little effort as possible, who wait to be told or to be asked, and who demonstrate minimal initiative or creativity. These retailers want to know: "How do you motivate staff?" Because this seems to be such a challenge in retail, we included the question in our research interviews. Here are samples from the responses we heard.

Question: **How do you motivate your staff?**

Retailer #1:   *We don't have to. They like to come to work. They like each other and care about each other. We treat each other the way each of us wants to be treated. We don't have sales targets for our staff. They know we have to turn over inventory quickly. We talk about performance daily and weekly. Our business is built on relationships.*

Retailer #2:   *This isn't a problem. We believe in them. We teach them and give them lots of responsibility. We also give them freedom to be creative and have fun in the store. We help them set targets, we recognize them, and talk to them a lot.*

Retailer #3:   *It's easy. New products, new promotions, new systems, and an opportunity to constantly learn new things keeps them motivated.*

Retailer #4:   *On their first shift, staff are taught how to ... They agree to complete three workbook assignments to develop product knowledge. If they do not do it, they will hear about following through and doing what they promise "without compromise." Staff have training sessions and can progress through several levels of achievement and promotion, even though the pay differences are minimal. We track and measure everything. People get lots of feedback and they love working towards the targets. They also have fun working in teams.*

> *"The job of a manager requires but two basic talents... motivating and communicating."*
>
> **Lee Iacocca**

Question: **Why do staff stay with you for such a long time?**

Retailer #5:   *We have a relaxed family atmosphere. We respect the staff and trust them. We don't single people out for recognition. Everyone works hard. They love the variety and the product. They love treating people well.*

Question: **I see you are here alone. How do you keep up your motivation?**

Retailer #6:   *I can't get bored. There's too much to do. Today, for example, I'm doing the signage for the window display. I have some customers I must call about their merchandise. I want to ask one of our suppliers a question about cleaning. We are part of a fashion show for charity and I'm thinking about what I will recommend for us to show. I was actually too busy to be on the planning committee for it but the owner asked if I wanted to be.*

MOTIVATION FROM A RESEARCHER'S POINT OF VIEW

The Theory

Frederich Herzberg, one of the many researchers fascinated by the subject of motivation, asked employees in different types of work: "What makes you want to work?" He found (as did many others after him) that the following factors call up energy and a willingness to work. As you read them, think about the quotes from the retailers and you will see the theory is alive and well in retail.

To the question "What makes you want to keep working?" employees responded:

Achievement   having a challenge to face, a problem to solve, issues to deal with or desires to fulfill

Recognition   being noticed as a person who is unique, valuable, important to others or important to the success of the work

The Work   doing activities and tasks that give satisfaction because of what they are or the way they can be done

Responsibility   being entrusted to do a desired job

Advancement Opportunities   having a chance to learn and/or earn more.

Are you surprised that money is not on this list? According to research, money in and of itself does not motivate people. It falls into a category of factors that have a negative effect on motivation. The following are linked to low motivation: too much or too little supervision; lack of satisfying interpersonal relationships; too much conflict; poor working conditions; too many or inappropriate work procedures; and salary perceived to be too low. Could any of these be sources of low motivation in your store?

How Can I Apply This Research in My Store?

How do you, as a manager, create the conditions that capitalize on these motivating features?

Achievement   The advice in Chapter 5 on developing performance expectations is not only about achieving store results: it is also about motivating staff. It draws attention to the fact that goals and standards motivate best when they are clear, challenging, personally meaningful, and when there is feedback on efforts and results. People don't exert themselves when they think the goals are impossible or the effort needed is too great. Clarify your expectations. Ask for staff input to be sure the goals are meaningful, challenging and possible.

Recognition   Earlier chapters on listening, acknowledging feelings, and feedback discuss daily ways of recognizing your staff. Recognition can be verbal or written, as tangible as a prize or as intangible as a cheer or a thank-you. The chapter on recognition and rewards provides many examples for recognizing performance.

The Work   All tasks have the potential to be satisfying for someone. A task (creating a visual display) might be motivating in and of itself, or it might be a stepping stone for satisfying other needs. Working in a team can motivate people with high needs for people contact, but be distracting or frustrating for others who like to work alone. Find out what people like to do best and try to assign work to match their preferences. Then, check to see if the work is valued by them.

Responsibility   Assign the work in ways that develop staff confidence and competence so that they can gradually handle more and more responsibility. Chapter 10, *Developing Staff Initiative Through Work Assignment,* provides useful tips on how to assign work and coach staff in ways that empower them.

Advancement Opportunities   A promotion of even a few cents an hour can be very significant. So can an opportunity to co-ordinate a project, represent the store, qualify for an honour, be sent to a course or conference, etc. Even though your business may not be large, you can still offer your staff opportunities for advancement.

Can you picture the face of the child first allowed to carry his plate from the table to the sink? Can you remember what it was like to be trusted to drive a car? And, how it was just as exciting to be allowed to drive alone at night?

You may read this and say: "I create challenging goals. I give a lot of praise and compliments. I try to give people the work they want to do. I give people responsibility. And yet, some of my staff are still not motivated. Why?" The answer may lie in whether or not you have matched what you are doing to motivate someone with what that person wants or needs.

Different strokes for different folks!

○ Perhaps the challenge you offer is not the one that gets Sam energized. Perhaps it's too much and Sam feels overwhelmed and disempowered. Perhaps it's too small and Sam feels undervalued.

○ Perhaps Sheila does not want recognition for the things you recognize, or perhaps, the way you provide the recognition is not valued.

○ Perhaps you have assigned tasks to match preferences, and now people are bored with their old preferences.

The more you talk with staff, the easier it will be to select appropriate ways to meet their needs.

Motivation Can Change from Moment to Moment

There are many variables at play at any one time and you are constantly determining which has the highest priority. Let's look at a snapshot in time.

It's 12:30 p.m. on Wednesday. Mario is serving a customer who looks like he will purchase several items. He remembers that you asked him to rearrange the centre display table before his lunch break. His lunch break is scheduled for 12:45 p.m. Today, he is meeting his brother for lunch in order to plan his wife's surprise party on Sunday. Mario is juggling a lot of things at this moment.

○ lunch and food

○ making this sale

○ being with his brother

○ the party for his wife

○ rearranging the centre display

○ not disappointing his manager.

As a manager, you are not aware of all the events that Mario is trying to juggle. You simply observe his behaviour. Although you think Mario is generally focused and able to give his full attention to the customer, today you observe him to be rushed, distracted and a little abrupt. What would you conclude about his motivation? What options would you have? What would you do?

Tapping into someone's motivation is not a one time thing. You will always be asking: "What specifically energizes, calls up willingness, desire and enthusiasm in this person at this time?"

Maslow's theory of motivation helps us understand the process of changing motivation by thinking in terms of a hierarchy of needs.

Hierarchy of Internal Needs That Drive Behaviour

When Abraham Maslow wrote about motivation in the 1950s, the debate focused on: Which was better, the carrot or the stick. Maslow provides more useful glasses through which to see the dynamics of motivation. He describes a hierarchy of human needs – internal "drivers" of behaviour.

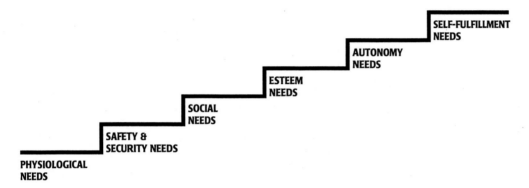

The most basic needs are **physiological** – to have food, water, shelter, warmth, and rest.

○ When staff say they need a coffee or lunch, they may be telling a physiological truth or expressing a preference. It's no accident there are mid-morning breaks in work in most industrialized countries. Companies, aware of the strength of physiological needs, have developed policies to address times when these needs could have an adverse effect on business. For example, many restrict buyers who travel to markets in different time zones from making large decisions on the day they arrive.

Application

Safety and security needs drive behaviour after physiological needs have been somewhat satisfied.

○ These include both physical and psychological needs for safety and security. Many of the former have been addressed through labour legislation. The latter include fear of ridicule, humiliation or embarrassment. For varying amounts of time and degrees of intensity, many people feel they are at risk when they start a new job. It is hard for a new hire to ask questions, disagree, or advance opinions. These needs also influence the amount of initiative shown in places where the managers humiliate or threaten the staff. The latter fits with the old-time "stick" approach which can, for as long as the boss is present, produce performance based on fear of the real or psychological "stick."

Application: work climate

Teams

Recognition & rewards

Style 4 Management

Social needs, the need for belonging, emerge after the basic levels of physiological, safety and security needs have been relatively satisfied.

○ These needs are so powerful that the performance of even very industrious, committed people will decrease in the face of groups that openly or subtly limit productivity. The opposite is also true. When a group has high energy and commitment to goals, it is capable of achieving great results.

Esteem needs emerge after someone feels a sense of belonging in a group. He or she generally wants to be noticed as a unique person – recognized in some special way, respected, seen as useful, and/or admired.

○ When you say: "Georgina does an excellent job on receiving shipments," or "Hari is a good model of how to deal with families shopping with a toddler," you are providing recognition that addresses esteem needs. Recognition does not always satisfy esteem needs. It must be related to the specific area in which the person wanted to be recognized. When it is related a sense of confidence develops. "I can do this." "I make a difference here." "My contribution is valued by others."

○ These needs can serve your business (e.g. staff taking initiative and using their unique talents) or sabotage it (e.g. staff distinguishing themselves through disruptive behaviours).

The **need for autonomy** motivates behaviour after esteem needs have been relatively satisfied. These include the desire for independent thought and action as well as power to make decisions.

○ Delegate to highly competent staff. Use Style 4 management for staff who are competent and willing to take on responsibility and accountability. Groom the rest of the staff so that they can take on the tasks you delegate and be successful.

The **need for self-fulfilment** emerges when the previous levels have been satisfied.

○ To varying degrees, based on how satisfied we are on previous levels, we all want to become "more" than we are now: we want to develop our potential.

This theory says that until one level of needs has been somewhat satisfied, a person's behaviour is not motivated by the next higher level. Think of people who are so fearful that they refuse to try anything new. If this is happening in your store, ask yourself:

○ Is this important? Is it a general pattern or an isolated incident? If this is important and a pattern, then ask yourself:

    ○ Could the refusal to try something new be a signal of unmet safety needs? Is there something threatening about the store, the situation, the staff, or you, the manager, that prevents this person from taking a risk?

    ○ Could this be a signal that the price of belonging is doing things the way the group wants them done, and that someone could be rejected by the group for trying something new?

    ○ Could this be a signal of vulnerable self-esteem needs? Could there be a need for coaching, for support, for dialogue about the consequences of taking a risk and potentially making a mistake?

Match the Job and the Individual's Motivation

Every job has a motivational profile. That is, the nature of the job and its components will satisfy some needs and not others. When you know the motivational components of the jobs in the store, you can better select the right people to fill them.

Let's explore this idea using your job and yourself. To get a picture of the type of motivations your job will appeal to, answer the questions in the chart on the next page.

"Ability is what you are capable of doing. Motivation determines what you do. Attitude determines how well you do it." Lou Holtz, coach of Notre Dame

MOTIVATIONAL COMPONENTS OF A JOB

In the work that you do, how much opportunity is there for you to:	None	Very Little	Some	A Lot
1. direct others' work?				
2. influence others ideas and actions?				
3. interact with people who have influence (owner, manager, key clients, suppliers)?				
4. become visible and highly regarded?				
5. work with others?				
6. develop friendly relationships?				
7. be with nice people who get along?				
8. help other people?				
9. care for other people?				
10. decide on your own methods for doing the work, and control the timing of it?				
11. take responsibility for planning?				
12. create something special?				
13. determine your personal goals?				
14. receive feedback on your performance?				

As you look at where you have placed check marks and the overall pattern, you will see a motivational profile of your job related to three needs identified by researcher David McClelland and his associates.

Power needs – people are motivated by the need to have influence, be included among decision makers and to have input, if not total authority, in decision-making.

Affiliation needs – people are motivated by social needs for contact and relationships.

Achievement needs – people are motivated by the need to achieve goals and accomplish things. They need to do things to a level that matches their standards, or perform better than they did the last time.

Three Needs

Questions 1 – 5 on the questionnaire are characteristic of **power needs.** Questions 6 – 9 relate to **affiliation needs.** Questions 10 – 14 relate to **achievement.** Notice that #5 is important for both power and affiliation and the 10th item can be related to both achievement and affiliation.

If you answer the same questions again, but this time in terms of the value to you of each of the 14 items, you will have a profile of your job preferences. How important is it for you to be able to have each of the 14 items as components of your job?

MOTIVATIONAL COMPONENTS OF A JOB

How important for your job satisfaction is it for you to be able to do the following as part of your job?	Not very important to me	Somewhat important to me	Quite important to me	Very important to me
1. direct others' work?				
2. influence others ideas and actions?				
3. interact with people who have influence (owner, manager, key clients, suppliers)?				
4. become visible and highly regarded?				
5. work with others?				
6. develop friendly relationships?				
7. be with nice people who get along?				
8. help other people?				
9. care for other people?				
10. decide on your own methods for doing the work, and control the timing of it?				
11. take responsibility for planning?				
12. create something special?				
13. determine your personal goals?				
14. receive feedback on your performance?				

What is the pattern of your job preferences? Does it match the pattern of your job as it appears on the previous page? If there is a poor match, motivation will wane quickly. The jobs of owner and manager generally have variety and the diversity provides compensation for the items that the person does not like to do. Is this true in your situation? Do you find that you avoid the items from which you do not derive any satisfaction?

You can use the questions in the first chart to provide clues to the motivational aspects of any job. While you can use the second questionnaire for yourself and others, keep in mind that it provides only a rough snapshot. During hiring interviews, you can share the profile of the job with candidates and **discuss with them** what they think motivates them. Use these as tools, not as final truths.

It is important to remember and help your staff understand that:

○ every person has needs for power, affiliation and achievement

○ the strength of each of these needs is different in each person

○ your success in keeping staff motivated will depend on the opportunities you offer that enable them to meet their needs.

Let's talk for a minute about **power needs.** Sometimes people think that a desire for power is wrong and should be hidden. However, the reality is that we all need power even though we may express the need differently. Here are some ways to respond positively to power needs:

○ give staff opportunities to influence your decisions and to make their own

○ make opportunities for staff to develop and use leadership skills

○ allow people to lead – chair meetings, coach others, deal with suppliers

○ provide opportunities for staff to be visible – represent you in the merchants' association, attend a seminar for you, meet your bank manager

○ structure your staff meetings so that people can become better informed and offer knowledgeable opinions.

How Does This Apply to Daily Operations?

Everyone has "down" times when their motivation is flagging. Aren't there some days when you are keen to get started on something and other days when you procrastinate on the very same tasks? Is it possible that your staff might feel the same way on occasion? Of course!

The more you are aware of the needs of your staff, the better you will be able to respond to "down times."

Marion is having an off day. You know she has a high need for achievement. Your choice is to say: "Everyone has off days," and leave her alone, or to try and tap into her motivation. Both can be useful choices. If you choose the latter, provide her with something new to learn, ask her to try something new, or provide a challenge to meet, a problem to solve, an opportunity to talk with you about plans, etc.

Simon, on the other hand, has a high need for affiliation. So, when Simon is having an off day or is frustrated, provide recognition, encouragement and support. Engage him in work that involves other staff. Giving Simon something new to learn will not be as effective unless it involves interaction with others.

CREATE AN ENVIRONMENT THAT RESPONDS TO MANY NEEDS

What is the bottom line? Create a rich motivational setting so that staff can find stimulation and satisfaction for the needs that motivate them. Look at the patterns in your store:

❍ Is your store a rich place for people with high affiliation needs? Does it develop and support positive relationships and teamwork?

❍ Is your store a rich place for people with high achievement needs? Does it offer challenging goals, high standards, and rewarding tasks? Does it provide feedback and recognition?

❍ Is your store a rich place for people with high power needs? Does it give staff a lot of information and empower them to provide input to decisions?

WHAT ABOUT YOUR MOTIVATION?

With all the responsibility involved in the job of being a manager, it is natural for you to experience disappointment, frustration and anxiety as well as excitement and happiness. Your motivation level may waver or slip backwards. The question is: "How do you manage **yourself**?" Are you the manager who deals with the challenge and bounces back quickly, or are you the manger who can be down for a few hours or even a few days?

Whether you are in a rut or on a roll, your motivation or energy level has a big impact on your staff. Your energy and motivation is contagious. You can pull them down or bring them up on top. If you pull them down, what will be the resulting impact on the customers? Can you afford to be down for two days, or two hours, or two minutes?

Here are three questions to ask yourself when you are facing a challenge and want to get out of the rut and back on top quickly. Ask yourself:

❍ "What else could this mean?" and you will be better able to change your focus to a more positive one.

❍ "What can I do to change this situation?" and you will look for alternatives in the one place that you really have control – yourself.

❍ "What am I willing to do to change this situation now?" and take action now.

SUMMARY

The assessment below summarizes the factors in the theories you have been reading. It can serve as a checklist of activities to create and maintain an environment in which your staff will want to work. Use it to get a snapshot of your role in motivation at this moment. You could use it again in six months to measure your progress.

> *Everything you do, everything you say impacts on the motivation of your staff.*

YOUR ROLE IN MOTIVATION

How frequently do you do the following?

1 point = rarely
2 points = sometimes
3 points = frequently

_____ 1. I am aware of staff preferences.

_____ 2. I am available to cheer on good days and to encourage on bad days.

_____ 3. I am as responsive as possible to their preferences.

_____ 4. I think about how responsive I am to staff feelings.

_____ 5. I think about the communications climate and whether it feeds people's need for affiliation and belonging.

_____ 6. I think about how I have designed the jobs and whether I can create a better match for staff.

_____ 7. I ask whether I am clear about my expectations.

_____ 8. I engage staff in setting challenging goals.

_____ 9. I think about the feedback I provide. Is it timely? What's the tone?

_____ 10. I think about the ways that I recognize staff and what else I can do.

_____ 11. I involve people in decision-making.

_____ 12. I think about how much responsibility I allow people to take.

_____ 13. I think about challenging goals to set for myself in terms of what I want to do to connect with the potential in my staff.

_____ 14. I offer staff opportunities to grow and develop their talents.

_____ 15. I listen to views and ideas from staff.

_____ **TOTAL SCORE**

HOW DID WE GET TO THE MOON?

One step at a time. You have made the time to read all or parts of this book. You are reading this now. You are willing and able to do the things that will help your staff support your success and theirs. One step at a time!

This whole book has been about motivation.

Start by giving yourself permission to do **something** without having to do everything!

1. MY CHALLENGING BUT ACHIEVABLE GOALS
    (be realistic – even a few will make a difference)

2. WHAT WILL I DO SPECIFICALLY?
    (what will the goals in #1 require you to do?)

3. WHICH OF MY NEEDS WILL THE ACTIVITIES IN #2 ADDRESS?
    (affiliation? power? achievement? other?)

4. HOW WILL I KNOW THAT I AM ON THE WAY TO REACHING THE GOALS? (what feedback will you listen for? ask for? when will you start monitoring?)

5. HOW WILL YOU REWARD YOURSELF?

YOU CAN DO IT – ONE STEP AT A TIME

Epilogue

The Art of Managing

There is no question that you are a juggler. You always have several balls in the air and several waiting on the ground. This is your life. Your carefully thought-out plans for each day are interrupted by one important issue after another. You are constantly re-ordering your priorities.

Learning something new often requires a temporary re-organization of how you invest your time. It includes willingness to devote time to your own development as well as to the learning of your staff. You and they will occasionally drop the ball. That's part of the learning process. It involves having patience for the mistakes that will be made and gleaning them to sharpen skills.

Visualize yourself with the other jugglers you have coached and trained. Along with you, they can keep the rhythm even when the occasional ball temporarily falls out of play. With your level of commitment, your achievements to date, and your retailer's zest, there is no doubt that the possibilities for success are endless.

We wish you every success.

THE FINAL WORD

.... is some personal advice to you from the successful retailers we interviewed. We asked them the question: "If you had one piece of advice to give to the retailers who will be reading this book, what would it be?".

○ Listen to people, staff and customers. Be open.

○ Define your vision and goals, them tell your team. Be generous of your time with staff.

○ Trust in your feelings, instincts, and gut reactions. Trust in yourself.

○ Hire the right staff. They are an extension of you, your store, your values and your image.

○ Invest time and energy in training your staff, treat them well and you will be successful.

○ Have real hands-on involvement. Walk your talk.

○ Make the store environment one where staff can learn and have fun.

○ Don't try to do it all. Give staff coaching and they will take on tasks you never imagined they could.

○ Care about people and success will follow.

Appendix I

DEVELOPING COMMITMENT TO SHARED VALUES

The purposes of the three meetings described below are to develop shared understanding among staff and between you and your staff about the values that guide the way daily business is done.

Values are sometimes called guiding principles. Use the term that you find most comfortable for you and your staff.

Step 1. Invite Staff to a Meeting

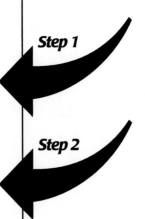

Invite staff to a meeting to talk about the way work is done and the values that guide how things are done. If your staff like to prepare for meetings or if you think it would help them, circulate pages 6 to 9 from Chapter 1 prior to the meeting.

Step 2. First Meeting
Gather Ideas About What Matters To Staff

The focus of this part of the meeting is to gather staff views about the values that are important to them at work. There are six parts of this meeting:

○ Introduction and purpose

○ Task to be done in small groups – respond to questions about values

○ Report group discussions

○ Clarify the items

○ Select priority items

○ Identify next steps

Materials Required

It will be helpful to have marker pens, flip chart paper or newsprint, and masking tape so that the ideas discussed can be recorded in a way that everyone will be able to see.

Time required: between 1.5 and 2 hours depending on the number of people and the pace of work.

Introduction and Purpose

Introduce the meeting by explaining that this will be a discussion in which there are no right or wrong answers. It will be an opportunity for people to talk about what matters to them in terms of the values or guiding principles that they would like to see at work. If you have not already circulated the information on values in Chapter 1 on pages 6 to 9, share it during the staff meeting.

Task To Be Done in Small Groups – Respond to Question About Values

To help staff become comfortable sharing their ideas, provide an opportunity for discussion in small groups of as few as two people or as many as seven. If you have six at the meeting, two trios would be best. If you have eight people at the meeting, two groups of four would be best.

Have two to three questions prepared. Give them to each group to discuss. Suggest a time of 10 minutes per question. Ask one person in the group to record the ideas of the group on each question. If there is no flip chart on which to record the ideas, the recorder can use ordinary paper. The advantage of recording on a flip chart is that everyone will be able to see what each group has discussed in an efficient way.

Here are some sample questions that staff have found useful to discuss.

What is important to you in terms of our product?

What is important to you in terms of our store?

What is important to you in terms of the way we do business?

What guiding principles or values do you think should direct how we treat our customers?

What guiding principles or values do you think should direct how we treat each other?

If you could make rules about how managers should treat staff, what would the rules be?

If you could make rules about how staff should treat managers, what would the rules be?

After 10 minutes, or earlier if the small groups seem to have stopped talking, ask people to share what they have been discussing in relation to each question.

Report Group Discussion

The purpose is to have everyone hear the ideas discussed in each small group and to build positive relationships.

Ask each group, one after another, to present the ideas they have been discussing in relation to each question. Focus on one question at a time. If you have provided each group with a flip chart and marker pens, have one person from one group read the list of responses to one question. Then move to the second group to hear its responses to the same question.

If the group has not written their responses on flip-chart paper, ask for a representative of the group to report the items discussed and you record them on a flip chart or in some other way that enables everyone to see them. If you do not have a flip chart, you can still record the ideas in a visible way.

Use marker pens and write one-two ideas per page on ordinary paper and post these on the wall or door so that staff can see them. Or, you can use marker pens on newspaper. Once there is marker-pen writing on newspaper, the printed articles fade into the background.

IDEAS ABOUT VALUES FROM GROUP 1

_____

_____

_____

_____

_____

_____

Post the flip charts on the wall so that you have a wall of ideas about values.

While people are reporting or listing ideas, don't evaluate them. To do so will discourage people from speaking. Also, ask others in the groups to refrain from criticizing or debating ideas.

Clarify the Items

Number every idea listed so that people can easily refer to them in discussion and in selecting the ones they favour.

Discuss duplicates, and ones that seem unclear. When everyone has finished contributing their individual responses to the questions about values, eliminate duplicates if the people who offered the ideas agree that the items are duplicates. If people who proposed the similar ideas think each idea is unique, note what is unique about each one and leave them both on the list.

Item 5 Meeting 1

Select Priority Items

The desired outcome of this stage of the meeting is to come to a list of 10 to 12 values that are important to most people.

Ask each person to **select the four to six** that they feel are most important to include in a list of important principles or values.

There are several ways to do this. Each person could write their choices on a piece of paper and hand it in to the manager. Instead of having to write out the ideas they have chosen, they can write the number of the item. Or each person could check off their preferences right on the flip charts. The former allows for more privacy and independent thinking. In the latter method, people might be influenced by what they see other people selecting.

IDEAS ABOUT VALUES FROM GROUP 1

|| 1._____

||| 2._____

|| 3._____

|||| 4._____

|||| 5._____

|| 6._____

| 7._____

卌| 8._____

Tally up the number of people who selected each idea.

DEVELOPING HIGH PERFORMING STAFF

Identify Next Steps

It is important to acknowledge the contribution that each person made and your appreciation of their willingness to participate. Close the meeting by:

○ making a commitment to write up the list in order of the 10 to 12 items most frequently chosen and to bring the lists back to the next meeting

○ schedule another meeting to discuss the list and relate it to daily practices.

You may want to offer to draft a values list that would reflect the ideas listed in a more readable way. You may want to ask for one or two volunteers to help you write up the list.

Step 3. Prepare a Draft Statement/List of Values

Work Alone or With a Small Group of Staff to Compile the List and Draft A Statement

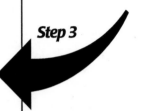

Step 3

Based on what you learned at the meeting, see if you can draft a list of key values or guiding principles. How do you feel about their suggestions? Are there items you do not feel comfortable with? Think about how you can discuss them with staff. How could the item be modified to be acceptable to you?

Hand out or post a draft, CLEARLY LABELLED "DRAFT" so that people can see it and think about it before meeting 2.

Step 4. Second Meeting

Bring the Values Down to Earth

Step 4
Meeting 2

There are two parts to this meeting. First, hearing each others comments on the draft. Then, taking a few items and discussing them in depth. The purpose in doing the latter is to help people see the relationship between the values and daily activities and interactions in the store.

Let people know that there are two parts to the meeting. Use up to half an hour for part one and about one hour for part two. The second half could be done over the space of two meetings.

Start part one of this meeting by reviewing the draft statement of values. Invite staff comments. They will offer changes.

List the ideas for change on a flip chart. This ensures the idea will not get lost.

After all suggestions for change have been listed, find out which ideas are important to the most people. A show of hands in response to the following question will tell you the priority of suggestions: "How many people want me to consider this change?"

Commit to considering the suggestions for change and to responding within a specific amount of time.

Shift to the second part of the meeting:. Focus on the meaning of the value in terms of day-to-day actions. Select two values from the list. Choose ones for which there were few suggestions for change. Ask people to talk for 10 minutes in small groups and answer the question: "What do we do that demonstrates this value in terms of the way we serve the customer and work together?"

For example, if treating everyone with respect is a value that you and staff want to highlight, ask staff to describe the kinds of behaviours they think would demonstrate respect and lack of respect. Continue through the list of values to get the daily behaviours people associate with the value statements. This will be an exciting, rich conversation.

See page 67 on receiving feedback

SAMPLE FLIP CHART		
Values Statement	How It's Demonstrated Daily	What We Need to Do Differently to Demonstrate It

Some tips for you. Refrain from giving negative feedback on what people say is important to them. Listen. Don't get defensive!

Close the meeting by thanking people for participating and advise them of what will happen next.

Step 5. Refine the Statement

Review the statement of values and refine it until you are satisfied it contains the important items for you and your staff. You will know you are on track when you say the words out loud and get excited by them. If you don't feel energy in the words as you say them, you will not be able to talk about them with conviction.

Step 6. Third Meeting
Plan the Next Steps

Invite staff to accept the revised statement as one that can be used for the next six months.

Suggest posting it on the bulletin board and/or using it to talk about ways of working again in a few months. Ask staff for their suggestions about how to use it.

Step 7. Reinforce the Values on a Regular Basis

It's human nature to forget, to be distracted from the values when challenges occur. Reinforce the values by continuing to talk about them, and by recognizing people when they exemplify one of the statements.

"Scott was a model for us all today. His handling of ... showed everyone in the store that we will go that extra mile to satisfy our customers."

Appendix II

DEVELOPING EFFECTIVE PROCEDURES

Procedures take the guesswork out of routine complex jobs. A procedure is a **clearly described method** for doing something that is to be **used by several staff, consistently** throughout the store. This is most useful for activities which are:

- routine, frequent, predictable tasks
- somewhat complex in terms of the detail or steps required
- related to security or safety
- time-consuming or problematic if errors occur
- done by different people

Procedures are helpful in areas like:

- Receiving a shipment
- Ringing up different types of sales
- Completing a return, exchange or refund
- Opening the store
- Closing the store
- Taking inventory
- Taking telephone orders or messages
- Dealing with theft or shoplifting
- Dealing with emergencies (fire, accidents, etc.)

Establishing effective procedures is an essential part of creating systems to support the efforts of your staff. They eliminate common errors by communicating a standard approach to the task. Effective procedures are one of the factors that make franchises like McDonald's and The Second Cup as successful as they are.

STEPS IN ESTABLISHING A PROCEDURE

1. Identify a task that requires a procedure

(e.g. unpacking a shipment of merchandise).

2. Decide on the most effective and efficient way to do the job.

Staff can often develop the procedure with or for you. They know the important details and the "dos" and "don'ts" that will make the procedure more effective. The advantage of working with staff is that people support what they help to create.

Questions such as the following can be very helpful in developing store procedures.

people support what they help to create.

○ What is the purpose of this activity?

○ What mistakes have been made in the past?

○ What have we learned from the mistakes?

○ How could this job be done simply and effectively every time?

○ What words will be understood by all staff?

3. Clearly define the procedure step by step and write it on paper.

○ Be specific.

○ Write down the sequence of steps that must be followed to do the job effectively and efficiently.

○ Include instructions to cover "what if" situations. Describe unique possibilities that may arise and what to do if they happen (e.g. if a statutory holiday occurs in the week, remember to note it on the report).

○ Include areas of caution about "what not to do" (e.g. don't return the full shipping document to the driver. Make sure to retain a copy for the store).

○ Outline approval levels that are required (e.g. if the manager is not available, the designated key carrier may authorize the document).

○ Specify the level of accuracy required (The bank deposit must be balanced: The restocking form is an estimate of what we believe we can sell.)

○ Specify the level of completeness required (e.g. the last three lines of the refund form may be left blank if the customer refuses, but we must have a telephone number for the customer).

○ Specify the timeliness required (e.g. this document must be completed daily, prior to closing).

4. Draft the support materials or "tools" required, i.e. a form or report.

Would a checklist or posted set of instructions be helpful? Is a common form or report needed? Will an example, sample or illustration be useful? Where will we put the procedure so staff can refer to it? Make it as easy as you can for staff to remember and follow the procedure.

5. Communicate the procedure, explain the reasons for it, and give staff an opportunity to learn how to implement it.

Ask staff to test the procedure by attempting to follow the steps. Use their feedback to refine the process or the wording of the procedure. Ask for feedback on the support materials. Invite them to help you design a way to monitor the implementation and the impact of it. These conversations with staff are vital. They will help you develop effective procedures, and they will increase the amount of staff commitment to successful implementation.

6. Monitor implementation to ensure the procedure is correctly understood and followed.

In the fourth step, support materials or tools were developed. Asking staff to note the time a procedure is started and the time it is finished could provide important information for planning. For the first month, it may be useful to have a checklist of the steps on which staff would indicate problems or suggestions.

Announcing a procedure and explaining it does not ensure that it will be used consistently. Give staff time to practise. Learning a new procedure takes time, especially if they only use the procedure once a month. Build in a process for tracking the use of the new procedure. It may be as simple as paying close attention to the way the activity (e.g. receiving shipments) is handled for a while.

7. Monitor implementation to assess whether the procedure is accomplishing what it is supposed to do.

Have the mistakes that were made before the procedure was introduced been eliminated? Are there new mistakes? Is it saving time? Are staff satisfied that the procedure is supporting the success of the store? Do they have suggestions for improving it.

8. Recognize staff for using it.

The new procedure will be adopted more quickly and more consistently if you recognize and appreciate the staff for using it.

AUTHORS' TOP CHOICE READING

Currie, Marilyn, <u>Achieving Customer Loyalty.</u> Toronto: Retail Learning Initiative, 1996.
(A how-to manual written specifically for the small and medium size retailer.)

Desatnick, Robert, <u>Managing to Keep the Customer.</u> San Francisco: Jossey-Bass, 1987.
(This book, written by the Vice President of Human Resources for McDonald's, provides practical suggestions on human resources management by a retailer.)

Gerber, Michael E., <u>The E-Myth Revisited: Why Most Small Businesses Don't Work and What To Do About It.</u> New York: Harper Collins, 1995.
(This fascinating book speaks to the small retailer. Join Sarah and her coach as she moves from solo entrepeneur to successful retailer, turning her store into a well-run, profit-making operation.)

Hyler, Bracey, John Rosenblum et al., <u>Managing From the Heart.</u> New York: Dell Books,Bantam-Doubleday Publishing, 1993.
(A story about a manager, outlining a beautiful philosophy for managing staff.)

Kent, Robert H., <u>25 Steps to Getting Performance Problems off Your Desk ... And Out of Your Life!.</u> Scarborough: Prentice-Hall Canada Inc, 1986.
(A hands-on practical guide about what to do if...!)

Lawhon, John, <u>Selling Retail.</u> Tulsa: J. Franklin, 1986.
(A step-by-step approach to sales, illustrated with a wealth of sample conversations.)

Nelson, Bob, <u>1001 Ways to Reward Employees.</u> New York: Workman, 1993.
(There are many inexpensive approaches for you to consider.)

Pfeiffer & Company International Publishers, in St. Catherine's, Ontario, at (905) 704-0406 provides catalogues of books, tapes and training materials in the area of human resources management.

Bibliography

Albrecht, Karl and Ron Zemke, Service America: Doing Business in the New Economy. Chicago: Dow Jones-Irvin, 1985.

Anderson, Kristin and Ron Zemke, Delivering Knock Your Socks Off Service. Toronto: AMACOM, 1991.

Band, William A., Touchstones: Ten New Ideas Revolutionizing Business. New York: John Wiley & Sons, 1994.

Belasco, James, and Ralph Stayer, Flight of the Buffalo: Soaring to Excellence, Learning to Let Employees Lead. New York: Warner Books Inc., 1994.

Bell, Chip R. and Ron Zemke, Managing Knock Your Socks Off Service. Toronto: AMACOM, 1992.

Blanchard, Ken and Spencer Johnson, The One Minute Manager – The Quickest Way to Increase Your Own Prosperity. New York: Berkley Books, 1981.

Block, Peter, The Empowered Manager. San Francisco: Jossey-Bass Publishers, 1987.

Collins, Eliza, ed., The Executive Dilemma: Handling People Problems at Work. New York: John Wiley & Sons, 1985.

Covey, Stephen R., Principle-Centred Leadership. New York: Simon & Schuster, 1992.

Covey, Stephen R., The Seven Habits of Highly Effective People. New York: Simon & Schuster, 1989.

Crosby, Philip B., Running Things – The Art of Making Things Happen. Scarborough, Ontario: New American Library, 1986.

Currie, Marilyn, Achieving Customer Loyalty. Toronto: Retail Learning Initiative, 1996.

Currie, Marilyn, Achieving Customer Loyalty: A Retailer's Guide to Creating and Sustaining a Service Strategy. Toronto: Retail Learning Initiative, 1996.

de Geus, Arie, "Planning as Learning", Harvard Business Review. March/April 1988.

DePree, Max, <u>Leadership is an Art.</u> New York: Doubleday, 1989.

Desatnick, Robert, <u>Managing to Keep the Customer.</u> San Francisco: Jossey-Bass, 1987.

Fisher, Roger and William Ury, <u>Getting to Yes- Negotiating Agreement Without Giving In.</u> New York: Houghton Mifflin, 1981.

Gerber, Michael E., <u>The E-Myth Revisited: Why Most Small Businesses Don't Work and What To Do About It.</u> New York: Harper Collins, 1995.

Hersey, P., and Blanchard, K., <u>Management of Organizational Behaviour: Utilizing Human Resources.</u> Toronto: Prentice-Hall, 1976.

Herzberg, Frederich, "One More Time: How Do You Motivate Employees", <u>Harvard Business Review 46 (1),</u> 1967.

Hyler, Bracey, John Rosenblum et al., <u>Managing From the Heart.</u> New York: Dell Books, Bantam-Doubleday Publishing, 1993.

Katzenbach, Jon and Douglas Smith, <u>The Wisdom of Teams: Creating the High - Performing Organization.</u> Cambridge: Harvard Business School Press, 1993.

Kent, Robert H., <u>25 Steps to Getting Performance Problems off Your Desk ... And Out of Your Life!.</u> Scarborough: Prentice-Hall Canada Inc, 1986.

Kneider, Albert, <u>Retailing Back to Basics.</u> Englewood Cliffs: Prentice-Hall, 1993.

Lawhon, John, <u>Selling Retail.</u> Tulsa: J. Franklin, 1986.

Le Boeuf, Michael, <u>The Greatest Management Principle in the World.</u> New York: Berkely Publishing Group, 1989.

Lucas, Robert, <u>Coaching Skills: A Guide for Supervisors.</u> Burridge, Illinois: Irwin Professional Publishing, 1994.

Lundy, James L., <u>Lead, Follow, or Get Out of the Way: Leadership Strategies for the Thoroughly Modern Manager.</u> San Diego: Avant Books, 1986.

Maslow, Abraham, <u>Motivation and Personality.</u> (2nd ed.) New York: Harper and Row, 1970.

Nelson, Bob, <u>1001 Ways to Reward Employees.</u> New York: Workman, 1993.

"The Research Report on Findings From the Canadian Booksellers Development Project." Toronto: Canadian Booksellers Association, March 1994.

Schatz, Kenneth and Linda Schatz, <u>Managing by Influence.</u> Englewood Cliffs, New Jersey: Prentice Hall, 1986.

Senge, Peter et al., <u>The Fifth Discipline Fieldbook: Tools, Techniques and Reflections forBuilding a Learning Organization.</u> New York: Doubleday, 1995.

Stone, Kenneth, <u>Competing with the Retail Giants.</u> New York: John Wiley & Sons, 1995.

Zemke, Ron and Chip Bell, <u>Service Wisdom: Creating and Maintaining the Customer Service Edge.</u> Minneapolis: Maclean-Hunter Publishing, Lakewood Books, 1989.

Acknowledgements

It is wonderful to have an opportunity to publicly thank the people who contributed in so many ways to the evolution of this book. We are grateful to have had a dedicated team of diverse professionals contribute to this book and to our learning.

Leslie Starkman, Education Co-Ordinator at the Centre for the Study of Commercial Activity, Retail Learning Initiative cheered us on, challenged us, coaxed us and did it all with a calm and caring manner. Her comments brought us ideas from her retail experience, her meetings with the Management Committee and a solid background in adult education.

The Retail Learning Initiative Management Committee and the members of the Booksellers Development Project Committee read and commented on each chapter at least once. Their thoughtful questions and practical suggestions supported our thinking so that we focused on providing the material that would be the most valuable to you, our readers.

The following successful retailers were invited to be part of the research for this handbook. Their "best practices" stories and information provided the life and energy that brings the management models and theories alive. The length of time their businesses have been in operation ranges from six to 148 years. The range of their individual experience spans decades, through economic upswings and downturns. Each one of them started out with one store. Some chose to stay that way and others chose to expand.

We are extremely grateful to each of them for their time, and more importantly, for the wealth of information they so willingly shared. Individually, each demonstrates a dedication, commitment and caring about their staff and customers that was a joy to experience.

This book would not have been possible without their valuable contribution.

FOLEY'S FURNITURE AND APPLIANCES
Collingwood, Ontario

GOW HOME HARDWARE
Bridgewater, Nova Scotia

KANE & BARON JEWELLERS
Mississauga, Ontario

KO'S OF MARKVILLE
Markham, Ontario

LICHTMAN'S NEWS & BOOKS
Toronto, Ontario

MARCI LIPMAN GRAPHICS
Toronto, Ontario

NORTH BY NORTHWEST
Cambridge, Ontario

SANDPIPER BOOKS
Calgary, Alberta

SPORTING LIFE
Toronto, Ontario

THE GAP
Toronto, Ontario

THE SECOND CUP
Toronto, Ontario

We wish to thank Ivy's Bookshop Ltd., Victoria, British Columbia and Simon Fraser University Bookstore for pilot-testing the material in their stores. Not only did they give their time to reading and applying the information, they provided detailed commentary on how to improve it.

Bill Tranter was involved in the initial focus groups and planning of the book. He wrote the early versions of many of the chapters and contributed significantly to our thinking.

We launched our thinking with a day-long planning session. We were excited by our conversations that day with: Jim Bangs of Kane and Baron Jewellers, Dan Benson of George Brown College Bookstore, Wendy Evans of Evans and Company, Gerry Ruby of Lichtman's News and Books, Marci Lipman of Marci Lipman Graphics, John Finlay and Jan Fralick of the Canadian Booksellers Association, Margaret Goulding of the Canadian Retail Hardware Association, Alicia Duval of the Retail Council of Canada.

We owe special thanks to our clients who, over the years, have taught us a great deal about managing people. The contribution of the people who, early in our careers, helped us to understand the challenge of retail and who introduced us to committed, energetic and creative staff deserves special mention. To Don Evans, we express our heartfelt thanks for teaching us.

David Rosenstein created most of the cartoons. His detailed reading of the chapters, his questions and good humour show through his very real characters. Two of Pat Cupples' cartoons were originally drawn for use with Tip Top Tailors and they continue to bring the amusement of our human foibles to mind.

We want to acknowledge the fact that we authors are essentially trainers and organization development specialists. We spend our time talking with people, not writing. We are grateful to Andrea Love for supporting the editing, providing thoughtful comments and producing the multiple drafts of each chapter. To Richard Symes at Caterpiller Press we say thank-you for patience and creative contribution to the look of this book.

For his understanding, good humour and support as this book overtook our lives, Diane expresses her appreciation to her mate, Jack Livingston. His generous spirit was in full evidence and played a major role in the work that went into this book. Dale wants to thank her husband Bill for all the ways he shows love and her daughter Johnna Lee, who taught her how to listen.

About the Authors

DIANE ABBEY-LIVINGSTON

President of **Diane Abbey-Livingston and Associates Inc.** based in Toronto, Ontario, Diane brings 25 years experience consulting with business, industry and not-for-profit organizations.

Diane specializes in designing and supporting effective learning – in coaching, in meetings, in conferences, in training sessions and in organization change processes.

One of her early experiences as a trainer shaped her approach. Working with managers at a conference centre, she noticed that they were quiet and reserved during the daytime training sessions and meetings. In contrast, during the evening, they came alive with energy, humour, insight and commitment to help each other. Same people – different settings. That event sparked her dedication to creating the conditions, in all settings, that bring out the best in people.

She has enjoyed the repeated opportunities she has had to provide organization change consultations, training programs, and coaching for Bell Canada, Big Steel, Goodwill Industries, Lotus Development Canada, Tabi International, Tip Top Tailors, over a dozen hospitals, voluntary sector organizations like the Canadian Cancer Society and the Canadian Diabetes Association, and government departments.

Training programs for which she is known and respected include: train the trainer, coaching, consulting skills, facilitation skills, managing change, problem solving, conflict management, and team building.

She is described as a lively, caring consultant, with high standards, who combines laughter with learning to support clients' in achieving their goals.

Diane has co-authored several books and articles of a practical nature. The most recent publications have been *Characteristics of Valued Workplaces: Snapshots from Hospitals* and *Managing for Learning in Organizations: The Fundamentals*.

A passionate believer in the benefits of voluntary action, she and her associates work to cross-fertilize the best of the volunteer world with the best from business and industry. She serves as a volunteer on several committees and boards of directors.

Diane was educated at McGill University, Ontario Institute for Studies in Education at Toronto University, and by the commitment of her early managers to her growth.

DALE D. BECKS

Dale is president of STRATEGIES FOR EXCELLENCE INC. a ten-year-old training and consulting company based in Hawkestone, Ontario.

Dale specializes in creating environments where people learn, change occurs harmoniously and teamwork flourishes. She facilitates the communication process effectively, and coaches executives who are challenged to build and lead teams in an ever-changing marketplace.

Clients such as Tip Top Tailors, Black Photo Corporation, Bank of Montreal, Royal LePage Commercial Divisions, Sunquest Vacations, SCIEX, numerous hi-tech companies and provincial associations report that Dale has unbounded energy and creativity, always delivers more than they expect is a caring change agent and an inspirational trainer.

Programs Dale has designed include: Management Skills, Recruiting, Interviewing and Selection, Performance Management, Designing and Implementing an Orientation Program, Sales Mastery Skills, Powerful Presentations, Effective Listening Skills, Facilitation Skills, Train the Trainer and How to Manage Your Boss.

Dale also has over 20 years of Human Resources Management experience in a wide variety of industries in both Canada and the United States.

Educated at the University of Guelph and York University, she is an active volunteer with national not-for-profit organizations and has held numerous executive positions with industry and trade associations. She is an avid photographer, gardener, birder, cyclist, skier and traveller.

PRICING AND ORDERING INFORMATION

Course Title	Workbook and Video	Workbook	Video	
Achieving Customer Loyalty	$99.00 ea. Quantity	$39.95 ea. Quantity	$75.00 ea Quantity	Total:
Developing High Performing Staff	$99.00 ea. Quantity	$39.95 ea. Quantity	$75.00 ea Quantity	Total:
Building a Winning Retail Strategy	$99.00 ea. Quantity	$39.95 ea. Quantity	$75.00 ea Quantity	Total:
				SubTotal:

Shipping and handling (up to 4 items: $5.00 – 5 to 10 items: $10.00)	
Plus 7% GST on products and handling charges:	
Ontario residents add 8% P.S.T. on Workbook/Video Combination **OR** Video only	

Name: _____

Company: _____

Address: _____

City: _____

Prov. _____ Postal Code: _____

Tel: _____

Total billing: _____

To order more copies of this workbook, or other items in this series, FAX or mail this form to:

Karen Madden
Retail Council of Canada
121 Bloor St. E., Suite 1210
Toronto, ON M4W 3M5
Fax: (416) 922-8011 or
Tel: 1-800-363-5125

Method of payment:

VISA ☐   MASTER CARD ☐   AMEX ☐   CHEQUE ☐

Card # _____ Expiry date _____

Signature: _____

Workshops
For prices and information on course workshops in your area, please contact: Leslie Starkman, Retail Learning Initiative
Ryerson Polytechnic University
Telephone: (416) 979-5000, (ext. 7203)

Retail
Council
of
Canada